TIKI

MODERN TROPICAL COCKTAILS

SHANNON MUSTIPHER

PHOTOGRAPHS BY NOAH FECKS

RIZZOLI
NEW YORK

New York · Paris · London · Milan

Dedicated to all those who dream of a better place—
and bring it to the people around them

First Published in the United States of America in 2019
by Rizzoli International Publications, Inc.
300 Park Avenue South
New York, NY 10010
www.rizzoliusa.com

Photographs by Noah Fecks
noahfecks.com

Pages 1, 6, 11, 20, 24, 31, 35, 45, 52, 57, 59, 69, 79, 84, 89, 91, 94, 97, 99, 100, 104, 107, 111, 116,
121, 125, 128, 133, 134, 137, 139, 143, 146, 149, 150, 156, 159, 161, 163, 185–87:
Styling by Christopher Spaulding, Reclaim Design NYC
rcdnyc.com

Pages 15, 17, 23, 29, 38, 41, 48, 62, 65, 71, 72, 75, 81,
108, 115, 166, 174, 178, 181, 183:
Styling by Rory Berthiaume
roryberthiaume.com

Designed by Jennifer S. Muller

2022 2023 2024 / 12 11 10

Distributed to the U.S. trade by Random House, New York
Printed in China

ISBN-13: 978-0-7893-3554-8
Library of Congress Control Number: 2018951630

CONTENTS

THEATER FOR THE SENSES

Mixing a fantastic cocktail requires a balance of art and science—knowledge of ingredients, flavors, and technique, and the skillful application of all three. Before being tasked with creating a rum-focused bar at Glady's Caribbean, I'd had very few craft cocktails made with rum, Tiki or otherwise. The latter I regarded with skepticism: While the restaurant's interior—trimmed by jewel-toned formica, adorned with lush foliage, and energized by upbeat island music—created the perfect setting, I knew one of the challenges the bar would face was the perception of rum as too sweet, and Tiki as tacky. I made it my mission then to present bright, crisp, and nuanced drinks not only to debunk these clichéd notions, but to show rum as an exemplary mixing spirit. I purposely chose spirits from our back bar that were delicious neat and did not need masking or enhancement by other ingredients. Within a few weeks, there was no question that this approach was well worth the effort. Rum flights sold at a brisk pace and guests peppered us with fascinated questions. Finally, and to my delight, a serious cult of devotees formed around our Mai Tai.

As I opened myself up to experimenting with Tiki recipes, my palate became more sophisticated, and my ability to craft more engaging cocktails, Tiki or otherwise, grew by leaps and bounds. I watched my confidence and skills blossom and learned to balance more complicated flavor combinations and more elaborate techniques, and to improvise—blending rums, mixing with cachaças, mezcals, sakes, and vodka to create more diverse and engaging drinks.

The key to making a truly special cocktail is to engage all the senses, and this is the heart and soul of Tiki. Tiki cocktails, and the experience around them, are intended to be transportive. Flavorful, richly layered, elaborately garnished, and presented in a deliberately theatrical style, when done right, Tiki is also the epitome of the craft cocktail. When made with quality spirits, fresh ingredients, and handcrafted syrups, and presented thoughfully, they deliver a full sensory experience, becoming more exciting and ultimately more memorable than a simple mixed drink.

Of the cocktail genres, Tiki is the most receptive to reimagining and remixing. Rooted in the desire to elicit surprise and delight, the best Tiki springs from a combination of personal experience, imagination, and craft. With all its history and tradition, the style, nevertheless, represents freedom and fun in cocktail-building, with invention and innovation at its heart. As you will discover, with a little creativity, skill, and wit applied, a Tiki cocktail can soar. In this book, I not only want to share recipes and know-how, but also to inspire the passion that exploring the unknown can bring. As you try your hand at making infusions, syrups, and cocktails, I hope you will notice your senses becoming more perceptive and that your willingness to try out new ideas grows along with your skills.

Shannon Mustipher

One
FOUNDATIONAL COCKTAILS

Most tropical cocktails, Tiki or otherwise, can trace their origins to the following cocktails. The common thread running through all of these are three key ingredients, referred to as the holy trinity: rum, sugar, and lime. These core elements—spirit, sweet, and sour—are the key to balance in any cocktail that falls outside of the realm of the Old Fashioned, Manhattan, Martini, or Negroni templates, regardless of spirit, complexity, or number of ingredients.

The techniques utilized here are simple and straightforward, making these recipes an ideal jumping-off point for beginners to develop their palate and build skills, while those already versed in rum can use the recipes to gain deeper insight into the character of bottles both familiar and new. Simple and straightforward, each preparation places the spirit as the main player on the stage. Trying a few rums in your favorite recipes will reveal the spirit's diversity and wide range of expressions.

BOMBO

The Bombo is essentially a predecessor to the Old Fashioned, which is a neat pour of spirit enhanced by the addition of sugar and aromatic spices in the form of bitters. Here, the spices play the role of the bitters, enhancing the aromas and adding a bright dimension to the rum. Try it with a style of rum commonly used when the drink was invented. Navy-style rum (see page 167) at 55 percent ABV or higher is a great choice, as would be an extra-aged or blackstrap rum, should you be inclined toward a richer, bolder cocktail.

Recommended spirits:
Plantation O.F.T.D. Rum,
Pusser's Gunpowder Proof British Navy Rum
Navy Rum Blend (see page 169)

1 bar spoon cinnamon syrup (see page 176)
2 ounces Navy-style rum

Garnish:
Whole nutmeg, grated

In a chilled rocks glass, combine the syrup and rum. Add a large ice cube and stir to chill. Garnish with freshly grated nutmeg.

CAIPIRINHA

Beloved of the late, great Sasha Petraske (who almost single-handedly rescued the lost art of pre-Prohibition cocktails from obscurity), the Caipirinha is something of a paradox—it is ubiquitous and yet elusive. Sasha's demonstration of the traditional preparation revealed to me how the version commonly served at many bars, including my own for a time, differed significantly from his. When shaken, oils from the pith of the lime skin are released, imparting an unwanted bitterness to the drink, obscuring the aromatic and grassy aromas of the cachaça, which is distilled from fresh cane juice rather than molasses. The secret to a stellar Caipirinha? It's built directly in the glass, uses granulated sugar in place of simple syrup (its texture gives an effervescence to the drink, whereas syrup would weigh it down with gumminess), and the muddling action focuses on the lime's flesh, taking care to avoid the bitter skin and pith. The result is a considerably brighter, crisper, and more refreshing version of the classic.

Recommended spirit:
Yaguara Cachaça Branca

2 to 3 lime wedges
1 bar spoon granulated sugar, or to taste (see page 175)
2 ounces cachaça

In a rocks glass, gently muddle the lime wedges with sugar, focusing on the flesh and avoiding the skin as much as possible. Add cachaça and 3 to 4 cubes of ice. Stir gently until the glass is chilled.

CANCHANCHARA

Delightfully easy to prepare and to enjoy, the Canchanchara is a simple beverage that, like many cocktails, has its roots in folk remedies. It was originally consumed warm, as a toddy, but is just as delicious on ice. If you enjoy various types of honey, this is a great drink with which to play around with your options. For the rum, I suggest using an aguardiente, a fresh cane spirit used in the traditional preparation, or a lightly aged Cuban-style rum for a more modern rendition.

Recommended spirit:
Diplomatíco Planas

3 to 4 lemon wedges
3 bar spoons honey
2 ounces aged white rum or aguardiente

In a rocks glass, muddle the lemon wedges with honey. Add rum and stir.

For a more contemporary version, add 3 to 4 ice cubes and stir until chilled.

GROG

When the British Navy adopted the rum ration in the 1650s, it consisted of half-pint servings of unaged, cask-strength rum served neat. Hampden Estate Rum Fire from the island nation of Jamaica is the closest example of this type of rum on the market today. In contrast to the hot, harsh, and rough seventeenth-century rums, however, it is very smooth. Life aboard the ships was no picnic and the ration was considered the highlight of the day and the best means of maintaining morale. Eventually, it became apparent that giving rum in this quantity to sailors interfered with their ability to perform their duties—hence the practical, and now iconic, addition of water, sugar, and lime to lengthen the drink. Floral, pungent, dark, and earthy Demerara rums, which the Navy came to prefer over other styles, make a historically accurate version of this drink.

Recommended spirits:

Pusser's Gunpowder Proof British Navy Rum
Hamilton 86 Demerara Rum

3 to 4 lime wedges
¾ ounce simple syrup (see page 175)
2 ounces Navy-style or Demerara rum

Garnish:
Bitters
Lime Wedge

In a rocks glass, muddle lime wedges and simple syrup. Add rum, cubed ice, and stir to chill. Garnish with bitters and a lime wedge.

TI' PUNCH

In truth, there is no real "recipe" for the national drink of Martinique, Ti' Punch, per se. It is meant to be built and enjoyed according to one's own personal taste, and it is reflected in the local saying, *Chacun prepare sa propre mort*, which roughly translates as "Each prepares his own death." In fact, on many French islands, be it at a friend's home or in a restaurant, the ingredients and implements are laid out for each imbiber to mix their own. Rhum agricoles, distinct from rums made from molasses, are distilled from fermented, fresh-pressed cane juice which enables the funky, vegetal, and fruity aromas from the sugarcane to remain intact in the finished product. Agricoles are also generally bottled at a higher proof, resulting in a bolder, more intense flavor. With this in mind, search for bottles that come in at 50 percent ABV or above. While this recipe calls for an agricole blanc, should you prefer an aged rum, try ambre or even vieux—in Martinique, the custom is to drink blanc in the afternoon and a Ti' Punch Vieux as a nightcap.

Recommended spirit:
Damoiseau 110 Proof Rhum Agricole Blanc

1 lime
1 bar spoon cane or simple syrup (see page175)
2 ounces rhum agricole blanc, preferably 50 percent ABV or above

With a sharp paring knife, cut a disc of skin from the lime about the size of a silver dollar, taking as little of the pith and actual flesh of the lime as possible (see page 182). In a rocks glass, muddle the lime disk with cane or simple syrup, then top with rhum. Stir well to mix.

Note: While ice is not traditionally used in the Ti' Punch—on the islands, it is considered sacrilege— if adding a few cubes makes it easier for you to enjoy, go for it.

FLORIDITA DAIQUIRI

Havana bartender Constantino Ribalaigua Vert made dozens of variations on the classic Daiquiri over the course of his storied career at the famed El Floridita bar, where he served many a Papa Doble to none other than Ernest Hemingway himself. Best known for his frozen and blended iterations, he made dozens of subtle adjustments to create different textures in the Daiquiri, always referring back to this simple recipe for inspiration. I recommend drinking it as quickly as possible—it goes down easily and begs to be followed by another. Important to note here: As with all the recipes in this book, I have listed the ingredients in the order of the build. In this drink, however, balance is make-or-break. By mixing the sugar and lime first, you can check that the sweet and sour balance is where you want it before adding the rum. Should you start with the spirit first, this will be difficult, if not impossible, to adjust.

Regarding the rum, I suggest making your first with lightly aged Cuban-style rum—if you have the means to get rum from the island itself, even better. Once you've gotten the hang of this recipe, I encourage you to experiment with a range of several rums across the categories. Behind the bar, we have what we call the "Daiquiri test"—if a rum tastes good in a Daiquiri, it will almost always be enjoyable neat or on the rocks as well as a solid base for a range of cocktails.

Recommended spirit:
Diplomatíco Planas

¾ ounce fresh lime juice
1 bar spoon granulated sugar (see page 175)
2 ounces aged white rum

In a shaker, combine lime juice and sugar. Stir with a bar spoon to mix. Add the rum, cubed ice, and shake vigorously—the shaker should be frosted and so cold that you can barely stand to hold it any longer. Fine strain into a chilled coupe.

Two
ESSENTIAL TIKI CLASSICS

Tiki is a sprawling category of cocktails with a no-holds-barred approach to ingredients and flavor combinations. The more evocative of the unfamiliar and unexplored, the better. Don the Beachcomber, who is legendary for his innovative and adept approach to creating unique flavor combinations, referred to his cocktails as "rhum rhapsodies." With this in mind, Tiki cocktails can have quite a few things going on inside of them, and it can seem intimidating to navigate all the nuances of aroma, flavor, and textures that can come into to play when you are getting started.

For simplicity's sake, we will start with twelve iconic cocktails that have shown enduring appeal over the years and often serve as sources of inspiration for bartenders looking to create a twist on a classic or an original. In addition to its use of rums and tropical juices, Tiki sets itself apart by doubling or even tripling up on the key elements of a cocktail—spirit, sweet, and sour—to create complex and memorable experiences in the glass.

Working and sipping your way through these recipes will make clear what distinguishes one rum from another and how each style behaves in a cocktail. The specialty syrups and liqueurs that give Tiki its unique character and personality are integral to the interplay between aroma, flavor, and texture when building balanced, nuanced, and delicious cocktails.

PLANTER'S PUNCH

This is, in essence, a Rum Collins. The ingredients are simple and echo an old Barbadian recipe for rum punch in rhyme form: "One of Sour / Two of Sweet / Three of Strong / Four of Weak." This is the holy trinity plus the addition of spice—here, aromatic spices and concentrated berry flavors courtesy of the bitters and grenadine. Early iterations of this drink used port or sherry, but eventually the preference shifted to funky, big-bodied Jamaican rums. I bridge the gap here by using a Jamaican rum that was finished in a sherry cask. For a more adventurous—and potent—version, consider Smith & Cross Jamaican Rum.

Recommended spirit:
Two James Doctor Bird Rum

2 ounces pot still Jamaican rum
¾ ounce grenadine
½ ounce fresh lime juice
2 dashes Angostura bitters

Garnish:
Maraschino cherries
Pineapple wedge

Combine all but the bitters in a shaker with cubed ice. Shake and strain into a Collins glass over cubed ice. Top with bitters. Garnish with maraschino cherries on a skewer and a pineapple wedge.

HALEKULANI

First served at the House Without a Key bar at the famed Halekulani resort on Waikiki, Hawaii, this is the perfect gateway drink for those who are new to or hesitant to try Tiki. Think of it as a punchier Whiskey Sour, with additional layers of fruit and spices to add a dash of beach-resort flavor. Consider, too, that this template works beautifully as a bowl or punch and will satisfy drinkers of just about any persuasion. To scale this cocktail up to any size, use the same ratios—here, 4:1:1:1:1—for the primary components. The grenadine and Angostura function like salt and pepper in that a little can go a long way. Start with 1 ounce of each, then serve with dashers of each to add a "pinch" more according to taste.

Recommended spirits:
Booker's Bourbon
Old Grand-Dad 114 Proof Bourbon

1½ ounces overproof bourbon
½ ounce Demerara syrup (see page 175)
1 bar spoon grenadine
½ ounce pineapple juice
½ ounce fresh orange juice
½ ounce fresh lemon juice
1 dash Angostura bitters

Garnish:
Dehydrated pineapple wedge (see page 184)
Dehydrated citrus wheel

Combine all in a shaker with cubed ice. Shake and fine strain into a chilled coupe. Garnish with a dehydrated pineapple wedge and dehydrated blood orange or lemon wheel.

PORT AU PRINCE

This is essentially a Planter's Punch (see page 19) made funkier and drier by using a style of Haitian rum similar to rhum agricole called clairin. Distilled from fresh cane juice, it has grassy, vegetal notes, restrained fruitiness, and, in some cases, a savory, slightly briny character—think of it as the mezcal of cane spirits. As with any rum punch, this drink is open to interpretation: Should you be in the mood for a Martinican Punch Planteur, replace the clairin and pineapple with rhum agricole and guava. To add your own personal twist to the cocktail, try an infused rum.

Recommended spirits:
Clairin Sajous
Hamilton 151 Overproof Demerara Rum

2 ounces clairin
¼ ounce overproof or Demerara rum
¾ ounce falernum (see page 171)
½ ounce pineapple juice
¼ ounce grenadine
¾ ounce fresh lime juice
6 drops Bittermens 'Elemakule Tiki Bitters

Garnish:
Whole nutmeg, grated
Orange zest

Combine all ingredients in a shaker with ice. Shake and strain into a Collins glass filled with crushed ice. Garnish with freshly grated nutmeg and a strip of orange zest.

ZOMBIE

There is an adage in Tiki—what one rum can do, two can do better—and Don the Beachcomber's classic Zombie takes full advantage of the range of flavors offered by the *three* rums called for here. Pot still Jamaican rum—known for its distinctive funk— brings enticing floral notes to the nose, while the soft, round, and buttery notes of the Trinidadian rum serve as a grounding element and foil for the bright citrus notes in the falernum. Angostura bitters and Pernod come together to bring a herbal and savory dimension to the cocktail, while 151-proof Demerara rum brings dark, gritty substance and a piquant punchiness that sends a proverbial jolt through the cocktail—strong enough to bring the dead back to life. To keep your house style secret, consider a custom blend (see page 169).

Recommended spirits:
The Scarlet Ibis Trinidad Rum
Hamilton Jamaican Pot Still Black Rum
Lemon Hart 151 Red Label Demerara Rum

1½ ounces aged rum
1½ ounces pot still Jamaican rum
1 ounce 151-proof rum
6 drops Pernod
½ ounce falernum (see page 171)
1 teaspoon grenadine
½ ounce Don's Mix (see page 176)
¾ ounce fresh lime juice
1 dash of Angostura bitters

Garnish:
Mint sprig
Lime wedge
Orange twist

Combine all ingredients in a shaker with cubed ice. Shake and strain into a Collins glass or Tiki vessel of your choice over crushed ice. Garnish with mint, a lime wedge, and an orange twist.

THREE DOTS AND A DASH

Created by Don the Beachcomber to celebrate the Allied forces turning the tide in the Pacific War, the name of this cocktail references the Morse code signal for victory. Bright, aromatic, and punchy notes greet you on the first sip, while concentrated berries and a dusky earthiness from the rums add an additional layer of aromas—dried lavender comes to mind. Honey and orange juice soften and mellow the cocktail, making it a bold, yet easy-drinking sipper. As with the Halekulani (see page 21), this classic cocktail also makes a delicious bowl for four or punch for a party.

Recommended spirits:
La Favorite Coeur d'Ambre Rhum Agricole
Hamilton 151 Overproof Demerara Rum
St. Elizabeth Allspice Dram

1½ ounces rhum agricole ambre 100 proof
½ ounce overproof Guyana rum
¼ ounce allspice dram
½ ounce falernum (see page 171)
½ ounce honey syrup (see page 175)
½ ounce fresh orange juice
½ ounce fresh lime juice

Garnish:
Pineapple leaves
Maraschino cherries
Pineapple wedge

Combine all in a shaker with pebbled ice. Shake and pour all contents into a double rocks glass and top with pebbled ice. Garnish with 3 pineapple leaves, 3 maraschino cherries, and a pineapple wedge on a skewer.

ROYAL BERMUDA YACHT CLUB

This is one of my favorite Daiquiri variations for those moments when I am in the mood for a subtle twist. Instead of sugar for the sweet component, two iconic Tiki ingredients come into play: Falernum, from which citrus oils, cinnamon, and clove lend a bright nose, and orange Curaçao, with its aromas of bitter orange peels, both complement and rein in the drink's sweetness. It goes back to the adage I like to fall back on when contemplating ingredients for a cocktail, "What grows together, goes together." Who am I to argue?

Recommended spirits:
Hamilton 86 Demerara Rum
Marie Brizard Orange Curaçao

2 ounces aged rum
¾ ounce orange Curaçao
¾ ounce falernum (see page 171)
¾ ounce fresh lime juice

Garnish:
Lime wheel

Combine all ingredients in a shaker with cubed ice. Shake and double strain into a chilled coupe. Garnish with a lime wheel.

MAI TAI

This classic is one of the least understood of the bunch. Essentially, it's a long version of the classic Holy Trinity template, with the addition of orange and almond syrups. Over time, a number of renditions have appeared—some involving blended ice or blue Curaçao—but without much of a relationship to one another apart from the name. The confusion over what makes a Mai Tai might be due, in part, to the fact that the original recipe changed when the rum it was based on, Wray & Nephew 17-Year, went out of production. Victor Bergeron (aka Trader Vic), who invented the drink, would later revise the recipe to use a blend of pot still Jamaican and Martinician r(h)ums to recreate the missing spirit. Whatever rums you select should display the same grassy, vegetal notes that characterize traditional Jamaican rums. These, along with the lime and mint, highlight the drink's bright and refreshing nature.

Recommended spirits:
Hamilton 86 Demerara Rum
Paranubes Rum
Marie Brizard Orange Curaçao

2 ounces aged rum
½ ounce rhum agricole blanc 100 proof
½ ounce orange Curaçao
½ ounce orgeat (see page 176)
½ ounce fresh lime juice, lime shell reserved

Garnish:
Mint sprig
Lime shell

Combine all ingredients in a shaker with cubed ice. Shake and dump into a double rocks glass. Garnish with a mint sprig and the reserved lime shell.

MISSIONARY'S DOWNFALL

I don't come across this drink often enough, and I think it deserves a hell of a lot more play than its more popular counterparts, the Piña Colada and the Painkiller—similar cocktails that push coconut cream and pineapple to the fore, while the citrus and rums brighten and spike what could be enjoyed as a sweet virgin drink. In the Missionary's Downfall, the coconut cream is replaced by apricot liqueur, giving us a significantly drier cocktail with a higher alcohol content and serving as an ambassador for Tiki to those who are disinclined toward drinking rum. Should apricot brandy prove difficult to find, consider using a dry apricot liqueur; Marie Brizard makes an excellent one, as does Rothman & Winter.

Recommended spirits:
Diplomatíco Planas
Rothman & Winter Orchard Apricot

1 ounce aged white rum
½ ounce apricot brandy
1 ounce Don's Mix (see page 176)
1½ ounces pineapple juice
½ ounce fresh lime juice
10 to 15 fresh mint leaves

Garnish:
Mint sprigs
Pineapple wedge
Lime wheel, scored

Combine all in a blender with pebbled ice. Blend on high speed until smooth, approximately 15 to 20 seconds. Pour into a hurricane glass and garnish with a generous mint bouquet, pineapple wedge, and scored lime wheel.

NAVY GROG

An exoticized version of Grog (see page 13), this is a case study in the art of embellishing a classic drink template—in this case, the Daiquiri, with rums typically used in Navy-style blends. The aged white rum's dry, crisp notes pair with the vegetal notes in the Jamaica rum, which are layered on top of the bright fruit and savory earth notes in the aged rum. A large specialty ice cube—the ice cone (see page 173)—gently mellows the drink, keeping it chilled for a sustained period as the rums bloom and the cocktail's flavors develop.

Recommended spirits:
Denizen Aged White Rum
Hamilton Jamaican Pot Still Black Rum
Bounty Dark Rum

1 ounce aged white rum
1 ounce pot still Jamaican rum
1 ounce aged rum
1 ounce honey syrup (see page 175)
¾ ounce fresh lime juice
¾ ounce white grapefruit juice
¾ ounce club soda

Garnish:
Lime shell
Miniature British flag

Combine all in a shaker with cubed ice. Shake and strain into a chilled rocks glass over an ice cone (see page 173). Garnish with a lime shell and miniature British flag.

JET PILOT

A classic from Stephen Crane's iconic Luau restaurant in Beverly Hills, California, this cocktail bears an uncanny resemblance to the Zombie (no coincidence, as the restaurant's bartenders were poached from Don the Beachcomber bars). It assembles a near identical list of ingredients to create a brighter, punchier drink. Lighter and more acidic Puerto Rican rum has replaced heftier Trinidadian rum; cinnamon syrup and grapefruit juice replicate Don's Mix. The falernum adds the last kick of acid and spice, unifying the core elements of the drink while acting as a meeting place for the flavors in rum, syrup, and grapefruit juice. While Crane was not as skilled in drink creation as Don the Beachcomber or Trader Vic Bergeron, the fact that his restaurant endures as a must-see icon speaks to his talent for creating a compelling experience that sets Tiki apart from other cocktail styles.

Recommended spirits:
Hamilton Jamaican Pot Still Black Rum
Ron del Barrilito 3 Star Rum
Hamilton 151 Overproof Demerara Rum

1 ounce Jamaican rum
¾ ounce Gold Puerto Rican rum
6 dashes Pernod
¾ ounce 151-proof rum
½ ounce falernum (see page 171)
½ ounce cinnamon syrup (see page 176)
½ ounce white grapefruit juice
½ ounce fresh lime juice
Dash Angostura bitters

Garnish:
Maraschino cherries
Pineapple leaves
Mint sprig

Combine all in a shaker with crushed ice. Shake and strain into a rocks glass over pebbled ice. Garnish with 2 maraschino cherries on a skewer, 2 pineapple leaves, and a mint sprig.

ISLE OF MARTINIQUE

Distilled from fresh-pressed cane juice, rhum agricoles can run the gamut of flavors, encompassing everything from funky, floral, and vegetal to fruity, punchy, briny, and savory. In Martinique, the only rum-producing region with an AOC system, the influence of terroir is on full display, making these spirits unique among the category by the way they show the character of a place. Styled after a Daiquiri, this drink is an accessible introduction to this style of rum. The restrained floral notes of the rhum and orgeat create a more nuanced nose, while light aging on the rhum allows the fruit notes to remain, with the addition of faint vanilla and white pepper for a longer finish.

Recommended spirit:
La Favorite Coeur d'Ambre Rhum Agricole

2 ounces rhum agricole ambre 100 proof
½ ounce honey syrup (see page 175)
¼ ounce orgeat (see page 176)
¾ ounce fresh lime juice

Garnish:
Dehydrated citrus wheel
Edible orchid

Combine all in a shaker with cubed ice. Shake and fine strain into a chilled coupe or Nick and Nora glass. Garnish with a dehydrated citrus wheel or edible orchid.

JUNGLE BIRD

Created at the Aviary Bar at the Kuala Lumpur Hilton, the Jungle Bird was among the last original Tiki drinks to appear before the genre—and all craft cocktails, for that matter—vanished in the wake of disco. Revived by Giuseppe Gonzalez, this drink gives a tropical twist to the Negroni by substituting fruit juices for vermouth. The rich gingerbread spices of Jamaican rum play off the herbs in the aperitif, while the vegetal funk of the Jamaican rum draws out the herbal notes. Pineapple juice delivers a soft, silky, and comforting texture, rendering the drink's edgier elements more accessible.

Recommended spirit:
Hamilton Jamaican Pot Still Black Rum

2 ounces pot still Jamaican rum
¾ ounce Campari
1½ ounces pineapple juice
½ ounce fresh lime juice

Garnish:
Pineapple leaves
Lime wheel, scored

Combine all in a shaker with cubed ice. Shake and strain into a chilled Collins glass over cubed ice. Garnish with 2 pineapple leaves and a scored lime wheel.

Three
SOURS

Many of my favorite cocktails are based on classics that utilize four or fewer ingredients, and as a result they often rely on one key element—be it the spirit itself, a bold syrup, or a flashy liqueur—to give the drink a unique character and personality. Sours are one of the earliest examples of craft cocktails, made possible by the introduction of the metal cocktail shaker in the 1850s. Based on a simple template— spirit(s), sweet, and sour—drinks known as "sours" are composed of the building-block elements that provide the foundation for more complex cocktails. A Gimlet is a sour made with gin; following the same template with rum gives us the Daiquiri. Given their simplicity, sours excel in those moments when you are in the mood for a straightforward, easy, and refreshing cocktail.

PARASOL

The serendipitous outcome of a gift of homemade banana jam, the Parasol is a lighter version of the traditional Banana Daiquiri, typically made with artificially flavored syrups and served frozen. The bright, fresh result here makes a strong case for keeping it simple. Reàl Ingredients makes high-quality infused syrups trusted by bartenders across the industry; however, Tempus Fugit Crème de Banane and Giffard Banane du Brésil—both liqueurs—are excellent choices in lieu of syrup should you prefer a slightly drier cocktail. For an extra-aromatic experience, use a St. Lucia-style spiced rum blend.

Recommended spirits:
Denizen Aged White Rum
St. Lucia-Style Spiced Rum (see page 169)

2 ounces aged white rum
¾ ounces banana syrup
½ ounce pineapple juice
¾ ounce fresh lime juice

Garnish:
Whole nutmeg, grated

Combine all in a shaker with cubed ice. Shake and fine strain into a chilled coupe. Garnish with freshly grated nutmeg.

Parasol Pop: Consider this fun, less-sugary Banana-Daiquiri-on-a-stick the perfect grown-up addition to a picnic or pool party. I prefer The Perfect Puree of Napa Valley's banana puree, as it has a texture that mimics ice cream—it's easier to handle if you let it thaw a bit in the refrigerator. In a glass or nonporous, nonreactive container, combine 12 ounces (350 milliliters) aged white rum, 3 ounces overproof Demerara rum, 2 ounces spiced syrup (see page 176), 4 ounces frozen banana puree (thawed slightly), 4 ounces pineapple juice, and 4 ounces fresh lime juice, and mix. Transfer to popsicle molds, insert sticks, and freeze for at least 24 hours before unmolding. Makes six 4-ounce pops.

TOUR LE CARBET

An agricole-based riff on the Royal Bermuda Yacht Club (see page 27), this drink is inspired by Martinique's black sand beaches and spectacular views of Mount Pelée, the island's most iconic natural landmark. Like that cocktail, the Tour le Carbet utilizes falernum, while Suze, a French gentian liqueur, assumes the role of orange Curaçao, lending citrus and spice notes softened by herbal aromas that amplify the grassy character of the agricole.

Recommended spirit:
Neisson Rhum Agricole Blanc

2 ounces rhum agricole 100 proof
½ ounce Suze
¾ ounce falernum (see page 171)
¾ ounce fresh lime juice

Garnish:
Lime wheel

Combine all in a shaker with ice. Shake and double strain into a chilled coupe. Garnish with a lime wheel.

QUARTERDECK

Navy-strength gins—higher proof, juniper-forward, and with a heavy emphasis on citrus oils—are a natural fit for cocktails, tropical or otherwise, that call for an abundance of bright, punchy notes on the nose. This is a Gimlet with an island flair and a great place to start for someone cautiously dipping their toes into Tiki. Green tea lends an additional herbaceous flavor, while yuzu accentuates the citrus peel and fruit botanicals in the gin. Marie Brizard's yuzu liqueur is remarkably bright, juicy, and fresh tasting, with next to no detectable sugar.

Recommended spirits:
Hayman's Royal Dock Navy Strength Gin
Marie Brizard Yuzu Liqueur

2 ounces Navy-strength gin
¼ ounce yuzu liqueur
½ ounce green tea syrup (see page 176)
½ ounce fresh lemon juice

Garnish:
Lime, zested
Dehydrated lime wheel

Combine all in a shaker with cubed ice. Shake and double strain into a chilled coupe. Garnish with freshly grated lime zest or a dehydrated lime wheel.

Variation: Add a fresh cucumber chip to the shaker to give the cocktail a faint honeydew-melon flavor and a refreshing crispness. If you go this route, garnish with another cucumber chip in place of the dehydrated lime wheel to add another fresh dimension.

ESCAPE TO FANTASY ISLAND

Bright floral notes, warming spices, and dusky, mellow fruit evoke the sensation of making landfall on a modern-day Eden before sampling the abundant fruit growing within easy reach. Robustly earthy rum and fresh mango come together to offer a rich and musky base on which to layer bright and punchy ginger and pineapple aromas. A fuller-bodied play on the Daiquiri that is equally enjoyable in summer as it is on a cool fall night.

Recommended spirits:
Plantation O.F.T.D. Rum
Giffard Caribbean Pineapple Liqueur

2 ounces Navy-style rum
½ ounce pineapple liqueur
¾ ounce ginger syrup (see page 176)
1 ounce mango puree
¾ ounce fresh lime juice

Garnish:
Dehydrated lime wheel

Combine all in a shaker with cubed ice. Shake and fine strain into a chilled coupe. Garnish with a dehydrated lime wheel.

LAKE AT NIGHT

Tiki is all about appearances and the element of surprise, so don't be fooled by the sapphire color of this cocktail. Reach for this one when you are in the mood to experience the unexpected. Rather than the sugary-sweet flavors you might expect from an electric blue drink, here you will find savory notes of smoked wood from the tea, while the cardamom imparts fresh, punchy alpine aromas with a touch of sweet resin.

Recommended spirits:
Monopolowa Vodka
Senior & Co. The Genuine Blue Curaçao

2 ounces smoked tea vodka (recipe follows)
¼ ounce blue Curaçao
¼ ounce honey syrup (see page 175)
½ ounce fresh lemon juice
2 dashes cardamom bitters

Garnish:
Orange twist or peel

Combine all in a shaker with cubed ice. Shake and double strain into a chilled coupe or Nick and Nora glass. Garnish with an orange twist or peel.

Smoked Tea Vodka: Steep 2 to 3 teaspoons loose Lapsang souchong leaves—or experiment with your own favorite smoked black tea—in 6 ounces hot water for 2 to 3 minutes. Drain the water (or enjoy a nice cup of tea) and transfer the wet leaves to a glass or nonporous, nonreactive container and add 25⅓ ounces (750 milliters) vodka.

Steep the leaves in the vodka at room temperature for 5 to 7 minutes. Drain and discard the leaves before the tea is over extracted; if left too long, the spirit will become overly tannic and woody as opposed to deliciously smoky. Decant into a clean container or bottle. Store in a cool place away from sunlight. The vodka will keep indefinitely.

DEATH VALLEY AT SUNSET

This is a smooth, tropical spin on a spicy Margarita. Papaya tempers the chile liqueur's heat, while savory avocado gives a gentle lift to the herbal and grassy notes of the tequila, making for a cocktail that takes you through the fire, so to speak, then greets you with a cool kiss on the other side. The avocado oil–washed tequila makes an excellent sipper on its own. If you are in an especially curious mood, try it as an alternative to gin in a Dirty Martini, with sherry or white vermouth in lieu of dry vermouth, and with brine or a pinch of salt in the place of olive juice.

Recommended spirits:
Blue Nectar Silver Tequila
Ancho Reyes Ancho Chile Liqueur

2 ounces avocado oil–washed tequila (recipe follows)
¼ ounce chile liqueur
1 ounce papaya puree
¾ ounce Don's Mix (see page 176)
¾ ounce fresh lime juice

Combine all in a shaker with cubed ice. Shake and fine strain into a chilled coupe rimmed with chile salt.

Avocado Oil–Washed Tequila: Combine 4 ounces avocado oil and 16 ounces (475 milliliters) tequila in a glass or nonporous, nonreactive container, and let steep at room temperature for 4 to 6 hours. Cover and transfer the container to the freezer for another 8 hours or overnight to let the oil solidify.

Remove the container from the freezer, then remove and discard the solidified oil and skim off any remaining solids. Double strain the tequila through cheesecloth before using.

ALMOST FAMOUS

Laura Bishop, Liberty Bar and Navy Strength, Seattle, Washington
Laura Bishop contributes this riff on the Paper Plane—bourbon, Campari, vermouth, and lemon taken in a fruitier direction by Hampden Estate Rum Fire, a high-ester Jamaican rum that boasts a wild riot of banana, papaya, and burnt molasses notes on the nose. Those flavors are tempered by gingerbread and spice from Aperol, while the yellow Chartreuse adds an additional layer of vegetal notes to play off similar flavors in the rum.

Recommended spirit:
Hampden Estate Rum Fire Overproof

1 ounce overproof Jamaican rum
1 ounce yellow Chartreuse
1 ounce Aperol
1 ounce fresh lime juice

Garnish:
Dehydrated lime wheel

Combine all in a shaker with ice. Shake to chill and fine strain into a chilled coupe. Garnish with a dehydrated lime wheel.

ISLA DE PIÑA

The beauty of the Daiquiri is that it is a fantastic template for a veritable universe of variations. This multilayered take on the classic touches on everything from bright citrus to dusky fruit to piquant spice courtesy of the pimento dram. The white rum, aged for up to six years and bottled at a higher proof, brings warm vanilla and white pepper notes and a plush mouthfeel to the cocktail.

Recommended spirits:
Diplomatíco Planas
Giffard Caribbean Pineapple Liqueur
Hamilton Pimento Dram Liqueur

2 ounces aged white rum
½ ounce pineapple liqueur
¼ ounce pimento dram
½ ounce passion fruit puree
½ ounce fresh lime juice

Garnish:
Pineapple leaves

Combine all in a shaker with scant crushed ice. Flash blend with a stand or wand mixer for 5 to 10 seconds and fine strain into a chilled coupe. Garnish with 2 to 3 pineapple leaves affixed to the glass with miniature clothespin.

CALIFORNIA CONDOR

Will Elliott, Maison Premiere and Sauvage, Brooklyn, New York
The California Condor is an unctuous pineapple Daiquiri variation, with no small amount of terroir and provenance. Saline, petrol, and the bright tropical citrus combination of pineapple, homemade lime cordial, and orange oil are all underlined by the slightest hint of spice and cacao.

Recommended spirits:
Santa Teresa 1796 Solera Rum
Hamilton Saint Lucia Pot Still Rum 8 Year
St. Lucia-Style Spiced Rum (see page 169)

1 ounce aged white rum
¾ ounce aged Saint Lucia rum
¾ ounce pineapple juice
¾ ounce lime cordial (recipe follows)
½ ounce fresh lime juice
8 drops mole bitters
8 drops Bittermens Hellfire Habanero Shrub

Garnish:
Orange peel

Combine all in a shaker with ice. Shake and fine strain into a chilled coupe. Garnish with the expressed oils of an orange peel.

Lime Cordial: In a medium saucepan, combine equal parts freshly squeezed lime juice and simple syrup. Bring to a simmer over medium heat and cook, stirring occasionally, about 15 minutes.

Four

LONG DRINKS AND COOLERS

In the mood for something easy? That is what long drinks and coolers—spirits lengthened by the addition of fruit and citrus juices, carbonation, or a combination of these elements—are all about. These are the lo-fi drinks of the cocktail world, easy to build in a glass or scale up by 4 to 6 servings, to pour from a pitcher for guests at home or bottled to-go for the beach or a picnic (or when visiting a friend who has yet to invest in a variety of proper bar tools). These are the recipes to reach for when you are looking to enjoy a simple drink, where the spirits are the focus and you have nowhere to be anytime soon.

MESSAGE IN A BOTTLE

Green vegetal notes, the hallmark of rhum agricole, receive a welcome lift from a kaffir lime leaf–infused rum. Like the skins of the fruit, the leaves contain aromatic oils, albeit in a concentrated, considerably more potent form; a little goes a long way. Its floral notes harmonize with those imparted by lychee, a light, fragrant juice with a clean, dry finish. Pungent and earthy ginger brings a layer of depth and complexity to the drink as well as a long, spicy finish.

Recommended spirits:
Diplomatíco Planas
Rhum J.M Blanc
Marie Brizard Orange Curaçao

1 ounce kaffir lime leaf–infused rum (recipe follows)
1 ounce rhum agricole blanc 100 proof
¼ ounce orange Curaçao
½ ounce ginger syrup (see page 176)
½ ounce lychee juice
¾ ounce fresh lime juice

Garnish:
Banana leaf
Pineapple spear
Kaffir lime leaf

Combine all in a shaker with cubed ice. Shake and strain into a snifter over crushed ice. Serve with bamboo straws and garnish with a banana leaf, pineapple spear, or kaffir lime leaf.

Kaffir Lime Leaf–Infused Rum: Combine 1 fresh kaffir lime leaf and 12½ ounces (375 milliliters) aged white rum in a glass or nonporous, nonreactive container. Let steep at room temperature for 2 hours. Drain and discard leaf before use. Decant into a clean bottle and store refrigerated indefinitely.

JADE MERCHANT NO. 2

Shochu is one of Japan's most popular distilled beverages, if less well known than sake. Like sake, it can display delicate floral notes on the nose, but with nutty almond flavors. Made from barley, shochu bears a faint resemblance to a soft, wheat-based whiskey and behaves in a similar fashion in cocktails. Aloe juice, which strikes a rare balance between vegetal freshness and silky creaminess, is supported by the addition of an avocado oil wash, bringing unexpected depth to a light and refreshing drink.

Recommended spirit:
Iichiko Mugi Shochu

2 to 3 sprigs fresh mint
2 cucumber chips
½ ounce fresh lime juice
3 ounces avocado oil–washed shochu (recipe follows)
½ ounce green tea syrup (see page 176)
¼ ounce aloe vera juice

Garnish:
Cucumber strip
Mint sprigs
Lime shell, scored

In a shaker, muddle mint, cucumber chips, and lime juice. Add remaining ingredients and shake to chill. Strain into a chilled double rocks glass lined with a cucumber strip over crushed ice. Garnish with a generous bouquet of mint and a scored lime shell.

Avocado Oil–Washed Shochu: Combine 8 ounces avocado oil and 25⅓ ounces (750 milliliters) shochu in a glass or nonporous, nonreactive container with a lid. Shake to mix, then let steep at room temperature for 6 hours. Transfer the container to the freezer for another 4 hours or overnight to let the oil solidify.

Remove from the freezer, then discard the solidified oil and skim off any remaining solids. Double strain the shochu through cheesecloth before using.

LITTLE GROVE

Batavia arrack, a cane spirit from Indonesia and funky ancestor to rum, was embraced by European drinkers soon after the Dutch began importing it back to the Continent in the 1600s, and became a popular ingredient in punches—the precursor to the modern cocktail. Fermentation starts with a red rice starter, giving the otherwise dry spirit a nutty and floral dimension. I have paired it here with ingredients that take full advantage of the arrack's unique ability to harmonize with a wide range of citrus and floral notes and to pull them into a delicious and cohesive whole.

Recommended spirits:
Batavia Arrack van Oosten
Iichiko Mugi Shochu

1½ ounces Batavia arrack
1½ ounces shochu
¼ ounce ginger liqueur
1 ounce rice-infused coconut water (recipe follows)
½ ounce lemongrass syrup (see page 176)
½ ounce fresh lime juice

Garnish:
Lime wheel

Combine all in a shaker with cubed ice. Shake and strain into a Collins glass over pebbled ice. Garnish with a lime wheel.

Rice-Infused Coconut Water: Combine 16 ounces (475 milliliters) 100 percent coconut water and ½ cup red, brown, or basmati rice in a nonreactive container. Refrigerate for 10 to 12 hours or overnight, then drain and discard rice. In an airtight container, the infused coconut water will keep for 1 week in the refrigerator.

SUNSET KID

Reposado tequila, aged in used bourbon casks, has a gravelly, cedar-toned character that plays up the floral notes of agave that are less detectable in unaged versions, where grass and herbal notes tend to take the lead. Those are supplied here instead by Cynar, an amaro whose botanical character is brought front and center by the infusion of artichoke. Blood orange brings a tartness that amplifies the bracing spice of cinnamon, while Fernet Menta, a greener, fresher spin on its darker cousin Fernet Branca, is a foil to the dusky wood and spice elements in the drink.

Recommended spirit:
Cazadores Reposado Tequila

2 ounces reposado tequila
½ ounce Cynar
¼ ounce Fernet Menta
¾ ounce cinnamon syrup (see page 176)
¾ ounce blood orange puree
¾ ounce fresh lime juice
2 heavy dashes Angostura bitters

Garnish:
Dehydrated blood orange wheel
Pineapple leaves

Combine all in a shaker with cubed ice. Shake and strain into a chilled pilsner glass over pebbled ice. Garnish with a dehydrated blood orange wheel and 2 to 3 pineapple leaves.

FLANEUSE

If the Planteur packed up her bags and toured the world, gathering various souvenirs in the form of flavors and ingredients from ports of call around the globe, she would look something like this. Rhum agricole and coconut lead the way with restrained fruit and marzipan notes, which are carried a few octaves higher by Becherovka, an elegant Czech liqueur infused with alpine herbs. Here, it also plays the role of aromatic bitters, tempered by light hints of honey. Amontillado sherry, a sweeter style typically enjoyed after dinner, brings a soft sweetness to the drink, while papaya adds earthen notes that bring it all full circle.

Recommended spirits:
Rhum J.M Blanc
Lustau Dry Amontillado "Los Arcos" Solera Reserva Sherry

2 ounces rhum agricole blanc
1 ounce amontillado sherry
¼ ounce Becherovka
½ ounce toasted coconut syrup (see page 175)
½ ounce papaya puree
¾ ounce fresh lime juice

Garnish:
Edible flower
Dehydrated pineapple wedge
Banana leaf

Combine all in a shaker with light ice. Flash blend with a stand or wand mixer for 10 to 15 seconds, to aerate and chill the cocktail. Pour into a chilled hurricane glass over ice and garnish with an edible flower, dehydrated pineapple wedge (see page 184), and a banana leaf.

CICADA

The Grasshopper, a rather hefty brandy-based cocktail made with heavy cream and liqueurs, is given a longer life span with herbal liqueurs and tropical juices. Light and floral pisco is grounded by aguardiente, a funky, vegetal, and earthy fresh-cane spirit similar to cachaça, albeit with less fruit. Together, they evoke a grassy meadow. Anise and absinthe take the place of crème de cacao, dialing back the sweetness in favor of the faint grassy notes found in dark, dry cocoa powder. Meanwhile, fernet mimics crème de menthe, with more savory herbal notes. Lastly, soursop, a lightly floral fruit juice that reminds one of pear crossed with pineapple, gets an extra bit of body from papaya, and together they stand in for heavy cream.

Recommended spirits:
BarSol Pisco
Paranubes Rum
Tempus Fugit Vieux Pontarlier Absinthe

1½ ounces pisco
½ ounce anise-infused aguardiente (recipe follows)
½ ounce green Chartreuse
½ ounce absinthe
½ ounce honey syrup (see page 175)
½ ounce soursop juice
½ ounce papaya puree
¾ ounce fresh lime juice
½ ounce fernet

Garnish:
Mint sprig

Combine all but fernet in a shaker with cubed ice. Shake and strain into a chilled pilsner glass over pebbled ice. Top with fernet and additional pebbled ice. Garnish with a generous sprig of mint.

Anise-Infused Aguardiente: Combine 2 tablespoons whole anise seeds with 34 ounces (1 liter) aguardiente in a glass or nonporous, nonreactive container. Gently mix, then let steep at room temperature for 24 hours. Fine strain and discard the seeds before use. Decant into a clean bottle and store indefinitely in a cool place away from direct sunlight.

TIGERSHARK

A double-hit of bright floral aromas—an exotic marriage of lemongrass and coconut—greet you on the nose, while nutty coconut oil enhances the toffee and caramel notes in the bourbon.

Recommended spirit:
Four Roses Bourbon

2 ounces coconut oil–washed bourbon (recipe follows)
½ ounce lemongrass syrup (see page 176)
½ ounce falernum (see page 171)
½ ounce fresh lime juice
2 dashes Angostura bitters

Garnish:
Edible flower
Dehydrated lime wheel

Combine all in a shaker with light ice. Flash blend with a stand or wand mixer for 10 seconds to chill and aerate. Strain into a snifter glass over pebbled ice. Garnish with an edible flower and dehydrated lime wheel.

Coconut Oil–Washed Bourbon: Combine 6 ounces unrefined coconut oil (unrefined is necessary for the desired effect; refined coconut oil is odorless and flavorless) with 25⅓ ounces (750 milliliters) bourbon in a glass or nonporous, nonreactive container with a lid. Shake to mix, then let steep at room temperature for 6 hours. Transfer to the freezer for 4 hours or overnight to let the oil solidify.

Remove from the freezer, then discard the solidified oil and skim off any remaining solids. Double strain the bourbon through cheesecloth before using.

JAVA JADE

East meets West in this play on a style of punch that was all the rage in eighteenth-century Europe. Batavia arrack, a slightly musky Indonesian spirit that is a precursor to modern rum, enjoyed widespread popularity for its ability to draw out and create harmony between the aromas in the spices and teas imported from the same region. Barrel-aged gin, reminiscent of genever—a malty, early style of Dutch gin that leans heavily on juniper rather than citrus and botanicals that are the hallmark of London Dry—adds heft and warm cassia notes. Grapefruit and coconut tie it all together with soft, tropical fruit, resulting in a richly layered drink that evokes the drams taken by seafaring adventurers of yesteryear.

Recommended spirits:
Captive Spirits Bourbon Barreled Big Gin
Batavia Arrack van Oosten
Giffard Crème de Menthe

1½ ounces barrel-aged gin
½ ounce Batavia arrack
¼ ounce crème de menthe
½ ounce toasted coconut syrup (see page 175)
½ ounce Don's Mix (see page 176)
¾ ounce fresh lime juice

Garnish:
Mint sprig
Lime, zested
Edible flower

Combine all in a shaker with ice. Shake and strain into a Tiki mug or hurricane glass over pebbled ice. Top with more pebbled ice, then garnish with mint, freshly grated lime zest, and an edible flower.

GOOD FORTUNE

Punchy and astringent, Szechuan oil is prized by cooks for its intensity and tingling, numbing heat. Famous for its cleansing qualities, it also offers floral aromas on the nose, followed by piquant fruits and the aforementioned heat, which gradually builds on the palate. Oils from the freshly muddled mint extend the cocktail's long, refreshing finish.

Recommended spirits:
Four Roses Bourbon
Pernod Ricard Pastis 51

Pastis
½ ounce mango syrup
5 to 6 mint leaves
2 ounces Szechuan oil–washed bourbon (recipe follows)
½ ounce lychee juice
¾ ounce fresh lemon juice

Garnish:
Mint sprig
Whole nutmeg, grated

Rinse a rocks glass with the pastis; pour in ½ ounce, roll it around the glass to coat the inside, then discard. Muddle the syrup and mint in a shaker, then add remaining ingredients. Shake and strain into the rocks glass. Top with pebbled ice. Garnish with mint and a dusting of freshly grated nutmeg.

Szechuan Oil–Washed Bourbon: Combine 6 ounces Szechuan chile oil—easily sourced online or from a specialty grocer—with 25⅓ ounces (750 milliliters) of bourbon in a glass or nonporous, nonreactive container with a lid. Shake to mix, then let steep at room temperature for 6 hours. Transfer the container to the freezer for another 4 hours or overnight to let the oil solidify.

Remove from the freezer, then discard the solidified oil and skim off any remaining solids. Double strain the bourbon through cheesecloth before using.

FIVE KNOTS

Gingerbread and spice notes from the Jamaican rum add a layer of intrigue to the restrained floral and vegetal notes of the rhum agricole. Cocoa and coffee come together to create a warm, savory, and slightly bitter palate, with the mole adding a punchy kick and a lingering spicy finish.

Recommended spirits:

Hamilton Jamaican Pot Still Black Rum
La Favorite Coeur d'Ambre Rhum Agricole
Tempus Fugit Crème de Cacao

1½ ounces pot still Jamaican rum
1 ounce rhum agricole ambre
½ ounce crème de cacao
½ ounce coffee syrup (see page 176)
½ ounce passion fruit juice
¾ ounce fresh lime juice
2 dashes mole bitters

Garnish:
Cinnamon stick, toasted
Whole nutmeg, grated

Combine all in a shaker with ice. Shake and strain into a rocks glass over pebbled ice. Garnish with a toasted cinnamon stick and freshly grated nutmeg.

MAGPIE

Unaged cachaça, just briefly rested to soften the brash, funky aromas of raw cane juice and saw grass, brings vegetal notes that dovetail with the aromas of papaya. Carrot lends an additional layer of similarly subtle earthy sweetness to balance out the bitter Campari. The result is a combination of unlikely ingredients that come together like a collage in which each element retains its individuality while forming a compelling whole.

Recommended spirit:
Yaguara Cachaça Branca

2 ounces unaged cachaça
¾ ounce Campari
½ ounce papaya syrup
1 ounce carrot juice
¾ ounce fresh lime juice

Garnish:
Edible flowers
Lime wedge, scored

Combine all in a shaker with cubed ice. Shake and strain into a chilled Collins glass over pebbled ice. Garnish with edible flowers and a scored lime wedge.

WINGMAN

Lo-fi meets high style in this nod to the Jungle Bird (see page 36). Browned butter–washing plumps up the rum—here, a funky, high-ester pot still rum that brings an extra oomph and roundness to the light, zippy cider component. You can always serve this (or any) cocktail in a glass, but if you are in a more irreverent mood and have good-quality canned pineapple cider, take a few sips of cold cider from the can, mix the rum, Campari, and falernum together, then pour the combined spirits right back into the can for a totally portable, slightly stealthy Wingman.

Recommended spirits:
Hampden Estate Rum Fire Overproof
Austin Eastciders Pineapple Cider

2 ounces brown butter–washed rum (recipe follows)
1 ounce Campari
½ ounce kaffir lime leaf–infused falernum (recipe follows)
Apple or pineapple cider

Garnish:
Pineapple leaves

Combine first three ingredients in a mixing glass with light ice and stir briefly to chill and dilute. In a rocks glass, pour over a large ice cube, top with cider, and garnish with fresh pineapple leaves.

Browned Butter–Washed Rum: In a small skillet, heat 6 ounces of unsalted butter over medium heat until it melts. Continue to cook, swirling the skillet constantly, until the butter foams and begins to turn brown and smell nutty; this may take a couple of minutes, but will happen quickly once it starts. Remove immediately from the heat and let cool slightly.

Combine browned butter with 23½ ounces (700 milliliters) of rum in a glass or nonporous, nonreactive container with a lid. Stir to mix, then let steep at room temperature for 6 hours. Transfer the container to the freezer for another 4 hours or overnight to let the butter solidify.

Remove from the freezer, then discard the solidified butter and skim off any remaining solids. Double strain the rum through cheesecloth before using, discarding any solids. Transfer to a clean bottle and store in the refrigerator for up to 4 weeks.

Kaffir Lime Leaf–Infused Falernum: Combine 16 ounces (475 milliliters) falernum and 1 lightly bruised kaffir lime leaf in a glass or nonporous, nonreactive container and let steep at room temperature for 2 hours. Before use, remove and discard the leaf and decant spirit into a clean bottle. Store indefinitely in the refrigerator.

LORIKEET

Inspired by the Jungle Bird (see page 36) and a species of parrot native to Australia and Southeast Asia, this loose play on a julep is the epitome of easy. Rye whiskey assumes the role of Jamaican rum, pulling the drink in a drier, spicier direction. Banana liqueur replaces Campari, adding a softer creaminess and a lighter, more tropical touch.

Recommended spirits:
Rittenhouse 100 Proof Bottled In Bond Rye Whiskey
Giffard Banane du Brésil

2 ounces rye whiskey
½ ounce banana liqueur
¼ ounce cinnamon syrup (see page 176)
1 ounce pineapple juice
¾ ounce fresh lemon juice
6 dashes Peychaud's Bitters
4 dashes Angostura bitters

Garnish:
Orange twist
Pineapple spears

Combine all in a shaker with ice. Shake and strain into a Collins glass. Top with pebbled ice, then garnish with an orange twist and 2 pineapple spears.

COCKPIT COOLER

The dramatic region of Jamaica known as Cockpit Country is characterized by steep-sided hills and hollows that capture pockets of warm Caribbean air. This creates a microclimate with an abundance of moisture in the atmosphere, which supplies the region with consistent, ample rainfall. Across the whole of the island, local produce is celebrated and freshly pressed fruit juices abound, including soursop, a large, prickly fruit prized for pleasant pear and pineapple flavors and immune-boosting properties. Allspice, wholesome carrot juice, and overproof rum (widely regarded as a folk remedy in Jamaica) only add more goodness to the mix.

Recommended spirits:
Hampden Estate Rum Fire Overproof
Hamilton Pimento Dram Liqueur

2 ounces overproof Jamaican rum
1 bar spoon pimento dram (see page 171)
¾ ounce toasted coconut syrup (see page 175)
1 ounce carrot juice
1 ounce soursop juice
¾ ounce fresh lime juice

Garnish:
Banana leaf
Whole nutmeg, grated
Paper umbrella

Combine all in a shaker with cubed ice. Shake and strain into a chilled pilsner glass or julep cup lined with a banana leaf over cubed ice. Top with pebbled ice and garnish with freshly grated nutmeg and a paper umbrella.

TIGER LILY

The Tiger Lily is ideal for those moments when you are in a mood for a fresh, floral daytime or brunch cocktail. Yuzu is one of the freshest, clearest expressions of citrus in a liqueur that I have experienced and it brings a delightful combination of crisp, punchy citrus and floral notes, while the soft, mellow botanicals from the elderflower liqueur add a hint of honeyed sweetness.

Recommended spirits:
Campo de Encanto Pisco
Marie Brizard Yuzu Liqueur
Giffard Fleur de Sureau Sauvage

1½ ounces pisco
½ ounce yuzu liqueur
⅛ ounce elderflower liqueur
1 ounce white grapefruit juice
½ ounce honey syrup (see page 175)
2 dashes Angostura bitters

Garnish:
Pineapple spear
Orange twist
Edible flower

Combine all in a shaker with a small scoop of crushed ice. Aerate with a stand mixer or wand blender for 10 to 15 seconds—the liquid should be slightly frothy. Strain into a hurricane glass over pebbled ice and garnish with a pineapple spear, an orange twist, and an edible flower.

ROYAL PEACOCK

Dani DeLuna, Brooklyn
Inspired by the Planteur, a Martinican punch of rhum agricole blanc, guava, and lime, this recipe gives sweet tropical fruit juices a hefty dose of savory. The mezcal's ashen, gravelly notes tease out the earthier dimensions of the agricole. Mango brings a softness and creamy texture to the lean spirits, while the shrub adds acidity and heat to mimic the chile-and-salt seasoning commonly served with the fruit.

Recommended spirits:
Neisson Rhum Agricole Blanc
Del Maguey Vida Mezcal
Giffard Crème de Fruits de la Passion

1½ ounce rhum agricole blanc
½ ounce mezcal espadín
½ ounce passion fruit liqueur
¼ ounce simple syrup (see page 175)
¾ ounce mango juice
½ ounce fresh lime Juice
1 dash Bittermens Hellfire Habanero Shrub

Garnish:
Pineapple leaves

Combine all in a shaker with cubed ice. Shake and strain into a Collins glass rimmed with chile salt over ice. Garnish with 3 pineapple leaves.

Five

BOLD AND FULL-FLAVORED

I like to think that my slightly unorthodox approach to cocktailing takes its cue from my approach to life in general. For as long as I can remember, whenever an opportunity to strike out in an unexpected—some might say slightly deranged—direction presents itself, I go for it. At age five, I jumped down a flight of stairs (much to my parents' horror) "to see what it would feel like," and I walked away without a scratch. Freefall ride at the amusement park? Sign me up. "Reverse firewalk" barefoot in the snow? Sure. Travel alone in a country where I don't speak the language? Give me a few hours and I will find a crew of friends with whom to share drinks, dancing, and a night out on the town. If it's already been done, it doesn't do much to attract or hold my interest. I love to play and create. Always have and always will. While the majority of these cocktails reference existing classics, they do so in structure or in regard to proportions of the components only. Beyond that, in these recipes I am reaching for spirits and ingredients in unique combinations that I seldom see applied in Tiki or tropical cocktails, classic or otherwise. Go for these if you are in the mood for a journey into the unknown—and be prepared to surprise yourself!

KINGSTON SOUNDSYSTEM

When I was approached to create a cocktail inspired by a reggae song, I chose "Skylarking" by Horace Andy. The instrumentation is spare; lyrics, simple and catchy. It's a song to nod your head or tap your feet to. That's the easy going spirit behind this jazzy reversal on the Jungle Bird (see page 36), in which that drink's ingredients are shifted to the opposite end of their respective poles—unaged rum replaces dark and tarry blackstrap; Suze, an aperitif based on gentian and other alpine herbs, takes the place of bitter Campari; and softer soursop becomes the base flavor in lieu of pineapple. Given the intensity of the other ingredients, the fact that the soursop shines through with a bright, eye-opening freshness is as pleasant as it is surprising.

Recommended spirit:
Hampden Estate Rum Fire Overproof

1½ ounces overproof Jamaican rum
½ ounce Suze
¾ ounce soursop juice
¾ ounce fresh lime juice

Garnish:
Dehydrated lime wheel
Pineapple leaf

Combine all in a shaker with cubed ice. Shake and strain into a rocks glass over cubed ice. Garnish with a dehydrated lime wheel and pineapple leaf.

KILL DEVYL REEF

Three iconic rum styles, each prized for qualities exclusive to their respective categories, contribute their signature aromas and flavors to this high-octane play on the Planter's Punch (see page 19). Heady floral notes intermingle with dried fruit on the nose. Allspice dram brings a savory element to the proceedings, backed up by the robust, dark, earthy notes of the Demerara rum, while passion fruit and honey add delicate sweetness to soften the drink.

Recommended spirits:

Hamilton 86 Demerara Rum
Damoiseau 100 Proof Rhum Agricole Blanc
Hampden Estate Rum Fire Overproof
St. Elizabeth Allspice Dram

2 ounces Demerara rum
½ ounce rhum agricole
½ ounce overproof Jamaican rum
½ ounce allspice dram
½ ounce honey
1 ounce passion fruit juice
¾ ounce fresh lime juice

Garnish:
Mint sprig
Whole nutmeg, grated

Combine all in a shaker with cubed ice. Shake and strain into a snifter or Tiki mug over pebbled ice. Garnish with mint and freshly grated nutmeg.

PLANK WALK

Warm, pungent spice greets you on the nose, followed first by musky, earthy notes courtesy of the papaya, then by light spice and citrus.

Recommended spirits:
Pusser's Gunpowder Proof British Navy Rum
Hamilton 151 Overproof Demerara Rum
Navy Rum Blend (see page 169)
Marie Brizard Orange Curaçao

2 ounces Navy-style rum
½ ounce overproof Demerara rum
½ ounce orange Curaçao
½ ounce papaya syrup
½ ounce cinnamon syrup (see page 176)
¾ ounce fresh lime juice

Garnish:
Whole nutmeg, grated
Flaming lime shell (see page 182)

Combine all in a shaker with ice. Flash blend with a stand or wand mixer for 15 seconds and pour into a brandy snifter or Tiki mug. Top with pebbled ice. Garnish with freshly grated nutmeg and a flaming lime shell.

MAIDEN VOYAGE

Before falling heads over heels for rum, genever and Old Tom gin, whose maltier and heavier styles eschew citrus and botanical flavors, were my cocktailing spirits of choice. Their robust flavor profiles can veer into whiskey territory. Searching for a way to marry my old and new flames, so to speak, I looked to two iconic Tiki drinks: the Mai Tai (see page 28), which I knew and loved to tinker with, and the Fog Cutter (see page 162 for Brother Cleve's remix), a classic I knew but regarded skeptically over its use of London Dry gin, which bore almost no resemblance to the styles I favored. Both cocktails bring two or more spirits into play, creating a broad spectrum of flavor on which to base the experience of the drink. I'd successfully mixed gin and cognac in the past, but now opted for Calvados, an apple brandy that is typically lighter and drier than Cognac, more acidic, and graced with floral and stone fruit aromas. If sourcing a quality Calvados for your home bar, I suggest looking for one that has not undergone "dosage," or the addition of sugar, which may add unwanted weight to the drink. Becherovka, a Czech liqueur, brings an additional layer of spice—think cinnamon and baked apples. A bourbon barrel-aged gin, drier than Old Tom and softer than genever, occupies a middle ground between the two. Finally, vanilla and orange Curaçao bring a silky mouthfeel.

Recommended spirits:
Captive Spirits Bourbon Barreled Big Gin
Lemorton Pommeau de Normandie
Marie Brizard Orange Curaçao

1½ ounces barrel-aged gin
¾ ounce Calvados
¼ ounce Becherovka
½ ounce orange Curaçao
½ ounce vanilla syrup (see page 175)
1 ounce pineapple juice
¾ ounce fresh lime juice

Garnish:
Lime shell, scored
Cinnamon stick, toasted

Combine all in a shaker with cubed ice. Shake and strain into a snifter and fill with pebbled ice. Garnish with a scored lime shell and toasted cinnamon stick.

POOLSIDE

I had the Piña Colada—all white rum, coconut cream, and lime—on my mind here, but wanted to dial back the sweetness a bit. Enter the baked-fruit flavors of banana. This adjustment draws out the vegetal and dry chocolaty notes in both the Navy-strength rum and cachaça employed here. Papaya brings an additional layer of depth to the drink, while the ginger adds a spicy kick and draws everything together for a long, layered finish.

Recommended spirits:
Plantation O.F.T.D. Rum
Navy Rum Blend (see page 169)
Avuá Oak Cachaça

1 ounce Navy-style rum
½ ounce aged cachaça
½ ounce ginger syrup (see page 176)
½ ounce banana milk (see page 129)
½ ounce papaya juice
½ ounce fresh lemon juice

Garnish:
Lime, zested

Combine all ingredients in a blender with ice. Flash blend for 8 to 10 seconds and pour into a swizzle cup (see page 180) or Collins glass. Garnish with freshly grated lime zest.

GHOST OF THE MARINER

Bitter and savory flavors—cacao, chicory, and smoky agave—stacked three-deep add depth and complexity to the base spirit while drawing out the wood, ash, and tobacco notes that the aging process imparts to the rum. Rather than use a rum aged for five years or longer, I let an infusion of coffee, cacao, and chicory draw out the wood, tannin, and spice notes. Meanwhile, coconut, honey, and orgeat—an almond syrup—add subtle nutty and floral notes that soften the bigger, broader dimensions here.

Recommended spirits:
Bounty Dark Rum
Yola 1971 Mezcal

2 ounces coffee, cacao, and chicory–infused rum (recipe follows)
½ ounce mezcal espadín
½ ounce toasted coconut-honey syrup (see page 175)
½ ounce orgeat (see page 176)
¾ ounce fresh lime juice

Garnish:
Whole nutmeg, grated
Cinnamon stick, toasted

Combine all in a shaker with cubed ice. Shake and strain into a Tiki mug over crushed ice. Garnish with freshly grated nutmeg and a toasted cinnamon stick.

Coffee, Cacao, and Chicory–Infused Rum: Using a funnel, combine 23½ ounces (700 milliliters) aged rum, ½ tablespoon finely ground coffee, ¼ teaspoon finely ground chicory, and ¼ cup raw cacao nibs in a glass or nonporous, nonreactive container (or add the spices directly to the rum in its bottle).

Let sit at room temperature for at least 24 hours to infuse. Decant the rum and strain through cheesecloth before using.

LAND OF THE LOST

Quality aged piscos are a best-of-both-worlds experience. The floral aromas found in unaged piscos, among the most delicate of any that you will find in any spirit, are further concentrated through the process of maturation, and even more enhanced by the vanilla and cassia notes imparted by the wood in seasoned barrels. Honey and guava, both quite floral in their own right, contribute additional complexity and a creamy, rich quality as well. Gently herbal aguardiente lays a meandering path to a long, satisfying finish. Absinthe adds a refreshingly herbal finishing touch, spritzed over the drink before serving.

Recommended spirits:
Alto del Carmen Pisco Reservado
Paranubes Rum
Ancho Reyes Ancho Chile Liqueur
Tempus Fugit Vieux Pontarlier Absinthe

2 ounces pisco amburana
½ ounce overproof aguardiente
¼ ounce ancho chile liqueur
½ ounce honey syrup (see page 175)
½ ounce guava puree
¾ ounce fresh lime juice
4 dashes mole bitters

Garnish:
Absinthe spritz
Mint sprig

Combine all ingredients in a shaker with ice. Flash blend with a stand or wand mixer for 8 to 10 seconds and pour into a hurricane or pilsner glass over pebbled ice. Garnish with an absinthe spritz and mint.

AGUILA DE DESIERTO

Inspired by the Mai Tai (see page 28), the Aguila de Desierto is a showcase for agave as a Tiki spirit, where reposado tequila's earthy funk makes a delicious change from sweeter, spicier rhum agricole. Orange Curaçao becomes tepache, a lightly fermented, cinnamon-spiked pineapple liqueur that brings a mild acidity and subtle, aromatic sweetness. Banana assumes the role of orgeat, swapping restrained fruit for marzipan, and the honey slides in savory umami notes.

Recommended spirits:
Tequila Tromba Reposado
Giffard Banane du Brésil

2 ounces reposado tequila
¾ ounce tepache (recipe follows)
¾ ounce banana liqueur
¾ ounce salted honey syrup (see page 175)
¾ ounce fresh lime juice
2 dashes Bittermens Hellfire Habanero Shrub

Garnish:
Lime wedge, scored
Cinnamon stick, toasted

Combine all in a shaker with cubed ice. Shake and pour all contents into a skull or tall Tiki mug, and top with pebbled ice. Garnish with a scored lime wedge and toasted cinnamon stick.

Tepache: Core and cube, but do not peel, 1 ripe pineapple, then combine with 1 teaspoon whole cloves and 3 cinnamon sticks in a nonporous, nonreactive container. Muddle pineapple and spices together, then add 4 cups brown sugar and muddle again, distributing sugar evenly. Add 8 cups water and stir to mix, then cover tightly and let sit undisturbed at room temperature for at least 8 hours or overnight. Stir again and add 4 cups lager-style beer (I like Narragansett or Red Stripe), then replace cover and let sit for another 48 hours. After the second day, the mixture should be fizzy, showing it has properly fermented. If not ready, let sit for another day. Remove solids and strain liquid into a clean bottle or container. Experiment with other spices, such as peppercorns, coriander, and grains of paradise for different effects. Keep in the refrigerator for up to 1 week.

MEDICINE WOMAN

Aguardiente is a fresh cane juice spirit from Mexico and Latin America. Until recently it was rarely seen outside of the rural communities where it is made in small stills, akin to the small-batch production of American moonshine. The earliest examples were rather hot and harsh. To mitigate this, infusions, mainly of anise, were used to soften and render the aguardiente more palatable. Thankfully, it is now possible to experience artisanal examples of the spirit that are not only smooth and easy to enjoy neat but make an excellent base for complex, multilayered cocktails. Each element here—mezcal, mango, and Cynar—express different dimensions of the core flavors of the base: fresh greenery, subtle fruit, and smoky spice.

Recommended spirits:
Yola 1971 Mezcal
Paranubes Rum
Ancho Reyes Verde Chile Poblano Liqueur

1 ounce mezcal espadín
1 ounce anise-infused aguardiente (see page 60)
2 dashes green chile liqueur
½ ounce Cynar
¾ ounce coffee syrup (see page 176)
½ ounce mango syrup
¾ ounce fresh lime juice

Garnish:
Mint sprig
Pineapple spears
Dehydrated pineapple wedge

Combine all in a shaker with cubed ice. Shake and strain into a Tiki mug over pebbled ice. Garnish with mint, pineapple spears, and a dehydrated pineapple wedge.

PEG LEG

Call this an iced hot buttered rum with a tropical bent. Creamy, nutty notes from the orgeat work in tandem with the sesame oil, which brings a fun, savory element to the bourbon. CioCiaro, a nutty and slightly chocolaty amaro, brings it all full circle, coaxing vanilla notes out of the Scotch.

Recommended spirits:
Old Grand-Dad 114 Proof Bourbon
Monkey Shoulder Blended Scotch Whisky
Tempus Fugit Crème de Cacao

1½ ounces sesame oil-infused bonded bourbon (recipe follows)
½ ounce blended Scotch whisky
2 dashes crème de cacao
½ ounce CioCiaro
¾ ounce falernum (see page 171)
½ ounce orgeat (see page 176)

Garnish:
Dehydrated lemon wheel

Combine all in a shaker with cubed ice. Shake and strain into a rocks glass over ice. Garnish with a dehydrated lemon wheel.

Sesame Oil-Infused Bonded Bourbon: Combine 6 ounces sesame oil with 25⅓ ounces (750 milliliters) bourbon in a glass or nonporous, nonreactive container with a lid. Shake to mix, then let steep
at room temperature for 6 hours. Transfer to the freezer for 4 hours or overnight to allow the oil to solidify.

Remove from the freezer, then discard the solidified oil and skim off any remaining solids. Double strain the bourbon through cheesecloth before using.

BROWN BOMBA

Get ready to play in the dirt! Grit and savory notes drift from nose to palate to finish in this slow sipper. Pot still rum gives off a floral funk that melds into the musky notes of the banana, which is subsequently spiced up by tangy tamarind. Honey pulls it gently back together, while the Irish whiskey and mole bitters bring spice and dry notes to the finish.

Recommended spirits:
Prizefight Irish Whiskey
Hamilton Jamaican Pot Still Black Rum
Tamworth Distilling Von Humboldt's Natur Wasser Tamarind Cordial

1 ounce Irish whiskey
1 ounce pot still Jamaican rum
¼ ounce tamarind liqueur
½ ounce honey
½ ounce banana puree
¾ ounce fresh lime juice
2 dashes mole bitters

Garnish:
Whole nutmeg, grated

Combine all in a shaker with cubed ice. Shake and strain into a hurricane glass over pebbled ice. Garnish with freshly grated nutmeg.

STRANGERS IN PARADISE

While the prevailing perception of mezcal is that it is smoky, gravelly, and even rough, in fact, it can also, by turns, be floral, fruity, silky, smooth, and refreshing. This recipe blends a mezcal espadín with a heavy dark rum, taking a cue from the blending of a heavy and light rum in a Mai Tai (see page 28). This version then takes an about-face from that original template, focusing on darker, savory flavors while pushing the citrus to the rear.

Recommended spirits:
La Favorite Coeur de Canne Rhum Agricole Blanc
Hamilton 86 Demerara Rum
Yola 1971 Mezcal
Giffard Ginger of the Indies

1 ounce rhum agricole blanc
½ ounce aged rum
½ ounce mezcal espadín
½ ounce ginger liqueur
¾ ounce macadamia syrup
¾ ounce fresh lime juice
⅛ ounce Fernet Vallet

Garnish:
Lime shell, scored
Mint sprig
Pineapple spears
Dehydrated pineapple wedge

Combine all but fernet in a shaker with cubed ice. Shake and pour all contents into a skull or tall Tiki mug. Top with pebbled ice and float fernet on top. Garnish with a scored lime shell, fresh mint, 2 to 3 pineapple spears, and a dehydrated pineapple wedge.

PEARL OF THE DEEP

Its "enchantment under the sea" name notwithstanding, this is a savory Tiki drink styled after Navy Grog (see page 32). Fresh floral aromas give way to zippy, tangy citrus, which works in tandem with the bright acidity of coffee, lending the cocktail a lively crispness. Pineapple further enhances all of these elements while adding a silky mouthfeel. Bright, concentrated berry flavors from the Demerara also lengthen this thread while grounding the drink in deep caramel and toffee notes and providing a long, sophisticated finish.

Recommended spirits:
Hamilton 86 Demerara Rum
Damoiseau 110 Proof Rhum Agricole Blanc

1½ ounces aged Demerara rum
¼ ounce rhum agricole
¾ ounce coffee syrup (see page 176)
½ ounce blood orange puree
½ ounce pineapple juice
¾ ounce fresh lime juice

Garnish:
Dehydrated blood orange wheel
Orange twist, scored

Combine all in a shaker with ice. Shake and strain into a snifter over ice. Garnish with a dehydrated blood orange wheel and scored orange twist.

MUTINY ON THE BOUNTY

When the Dutch began the spice trade, exotic ingredients and flavors were immediately and enthusiastically integrated into European drinking culture, which until that point had been dominated by beer, wine, port, and sherry. Spirits were less popular at this time, as the tweaks that made them more palatable to society's tastes had yet to be developed. With the addition of tea, spices, and citrus, a new beverage was born—punch. Here, gin's botanicals are enhanced by elegant Darjeeling tea, its citrus notes given a lift by the bright acidity of tangerine, and Jamaican rum supports the floral aromatics and concentrated overripe fruit flavors present in all of these.

Recommended spirits:
Hamilton Jamaican Pot Still Black Rum
Perry's Tot Navy Strength Gin

1½ ounces pot still Jamaican rum
½ ounce Darjeeling-infused gin (recipe follows)
½ ounce spiced syrup (see page 176)
½ ounce tangerine juice
¾ ounce fresh lime juice

Garnish:
Mint sprig
Edible flower
Lime wheel, scored
Dehydrated pineapple wedge

Combine all in a shaker with cubed ice. Shake and pour all contents into a Tiki mug and top with pebbled ice. Garnish with mint, an edible flower, a scored lime wheel, and a dehydrated pineapple wedge.

Darjeeling-Infused Gin: Steep 2 to 3 teaspoons loose Darjeeling tea leaves in 6 ounces hot water for 2 to 3 minutes. Drain the water and transfer the wet leaves to a glass or nonporous, nonreactive container and add 25⅓ ounces (750 milliters) gin, preferably Navy-strength, and stir to mix.

Steep at room temperature for 5 to 7 minutes. Fine strain and discard the leaves before the tea is over extracted; if left too long, the result will be overly tannic and bitter. Decant into a clean container or bottle. Store in a cool place away from sunlight. The tea-infused gin will keep indefinitely.

GOLDEN BARNACLE

Lush floral and fruit aromas of Jamaican and Martinican r(h)ums bloom on the nose, along with baking-spice notes from the allspice dram. Don's Mix—the celebrated blend of grapefruit, honey, and cinnamon—adds to the bouquet while contributing roundness and subtle sweetness to the cocktail. The dram reemerges on the last sip, adding depth and dry, elegant tannins to the finish.

Recommended spirits:
Neisson Rhum Agricole Blanc
Two James Doctor Bird Rum
Hamilton Pimento Dram Liqueur

1 ounce rhum agricole blanc
½ ounce pot still Jamaican rum
½ ounce allspice dram
1 ounce Don's Mix (see page 176)
½ ounce fresh lime juice

Garnish:
Blood orange wheel

Combine all in a shaker with 3 or 4 cubes of ice (light ice). Flash blend with a stand or wand mixer for 10 to 15 seconds. Pour into a rocks glass over ice. Garnish with a blood orange wheel.

MR. BODI HAI

Nathan Hazard, Coconut Club, Los Angeles, California
The Coconut Club's impressario offers his take on the Mr. Bali Hai, San Diego's contribution to Southern California Tiki culture.

Recommended spirits:

Real McCoy Single Blended Rum Aged 5 Years
St. George NOLA Coffee Liqueur
Giffard Banane du Brésil

1½ ounces aged rum
¼ ounce coffee liqueur
¼ ounce banana liqueur
½ ounce macadamia nut orgeat (recipe follows)
1½ ounces pineapple juice
¾ ounce fresh lemon juice
Dash Angostura bitters

Garnish:
Pineapple round
Pineapple leaves

Combine all ingredients in a cocktail shaker and top with cracked ice. Shake vigorously and pour all contents into a hurricane or pilsner glass. Top with crushed ice and garnish with a pineapple round and leaves.

Macadamia Nut Orgeat: Preheat the oven to 400°F. Spread 1 cup roasted, unsalted macadamia nuts on a baking sheet. Place in center rack in oven and bake just until fragrant, about 10 minutes. Remove from the oven, let cool, and transfer nuts to a blender or food processor along with 2 cups warm water. Blend on high for about 1 minute, or until well incorporated and frothy. Fine strain through cheesecloth or a chinois, then discard the solids and transfer the liquid back into the same blender or food processor. Add 1 cup sugar and a pinch of kosher salt and blend on high for about 1 minute, or until the sugar is fully dissolved. Fine strain into a glass container with an airtight lid. The orgeat will keep for up to 2 weeks in the refrigerator.

Six

FIERY, SAVORY, AND BITTER

Full bodied, substantial, and slightly brash, these cocktails lean heavily on ingredients and textures that cover everything from rich and creamy to dark, earthy, and gritty. Liberal use of spiced syrups, amari, and bitters give these cocktails unlikely and unconventional flavor combinations. These are the recipes to reach for when you are after an edgier, more adventurous drink.

HEADHUNTER

A boozy play on an iced latte with an "extra shot" of espresso in the form of Fernet Vallet—a chocolaty amaro from Mexico that is folded into the cocktail along with Cardamaro, which brings subdued caramel and hazelnut notes. Jamaican rum and mezcal come together like two sides of the same coin, bringing to mind the dark notes characteristic of a Guatemalan or Sumatran coffee. Red rice lends an additional savory nuttiness and a softness that bridges the gap between the spirits and amari.

Recommended spirits:
Del Maguey Vida Mezcal
Hamilton Jamaican Pot Still Black Rum

1 ounce mezcal
1 ounce pot still Jamaican rum
¼ ounce Cardamaro
⅛ ounce Fernet Vallet
1 ounce red rice horchata (recipe follows)

Garnish:
Mint
Orange twist
Flaming lime shell (see page 182)

Combine all in a shaker with a light scoop (less than half full) of pebbled ice. Flash blend with a stand or wand mixer for 10 to 15 seconds, then pour into a tall Tiki mug and top with crushed ice. Garnish with mint, an orange twist, and a flaming lime shell.

Red Rice Horchata: Toast 1 cinnamon stick in a dry pan over medium heat until fragrant. Let cool, then break into smaller pieces and combine with 1 cup red or purple rice, 2 cups whole almonds, 1 cup pitted Medjool dates, and 4½ cups (1 liter) boiling water in a large glass or nonporous, nonreactive bowl or container. Let steep at room temperature for 4 hours, then fine strain through a chinois and discard the solids. The horchata will keep in an airtight container in the refrigerator for 2 to 3 days.

SONG OF THE SIREN

I cannot resist drinks that fall under what I call the "shape-shifter" category, where the appearance, initial flavors on the first sip, and your first impression take an unexpected turn. This cocktail is one of my favorite examples of the type. Bright, fresh pineapple, its sweetness dialed back slightly by crème de cacao, slowly descends into grit and gravel imparted by rhum agricole from the flinty, volcanic soil at the base of Mount Pelée on the northernmost tip of Martinique. Braulio, an amaro infused with alpine botanicals that evoke fresh pine, comes together with yet another high-elevation element, mezcal espadín. The mezcal's soft fruit, vanilla, and cinnamon notes tie the cocktail together.

Recommended spirits:
Rhum J.M Blanc
Del Maguey Vida Mezcal
Tempus Fugit Crème de Cacao

1 ounce rhum agricole 100 proof
½ ounce mezcal espadín
½ ounce crème de cacao
½ ounce pineapple juice
¾ ounce fresh lime juice
¼ ounce Braulio

Garnish:
Banana leaf
Whole nutmeg, grated

Combine all but Braulio in a shaker with cubed ice. Shake and pour into a hurricane or pilsner glass lined with a banana leaf. Top with pebbled ice and float amaro on top. Garnish with freshly grated nutmeg.

MUERTITO VIVO

In an effort to create a simplified spin on the Zombie (see page 25), I sought out elements that could do double or triple duty in terms of supplying bitterness, as well as elements of citrus and spice. While allspice dram perfectly fills the bill on all counts, it is very dry. Without a juice other than lime to play against, it can exert too much influence on the cocktail, pushing it in an austere direction. Not very Tiki. Jägermeister, which is commonly thought of as a college-bar shot, is actually an amaro and becomes the unlikely star of the show here, providing savory cacao, crisp citrus, and bright spice notes.

Recommended spirits:
Flor de Caña 7 Year
Hamilton 151 Overproof Demerara Rum

1½ ounces extra-aged rum
½ ounce overproof Demerara rum
¾ ounce Jägermeister
¾ ounce Don's Mix (see page 176)
¾ ounce fresh lime juice

Garnish:
Cinnamon sticks
Edible flower

Combine all in a shaker with cubed ice. Shake and strain into a skull mug or chilled double rocks glass over pebbled ice. Garnish with 2 cinnamon sticks and an edible flower.

INFERNAL TRIANGLE

As the name implies, this drink involves sailing into uncharted flavor territories. A blend of agave and cane spirits are first layered atop a trio of liqueurs based on tropical fruits and spices, then paired with honey and pineapple, which gives this drink a soothing, easy-drinking character. The blend of smoky, spicy, and intense, concentrated berry notes, combined with cachaça's lushness—further amplified by the liqueurs and juices—results in an enigmatic and difficult-to-pin-down cocktail composed of a gaggle of unlikely but alluring bedfellows.

Recommended spirits:
Avuá Oak Cachaça
Del Maguey Vida Mezcal
Ancho Reyes Ancho Chile Liqueur
Giffard Banane du Brésil

1 ounce aged cachaça
½ ounce mezcal espadín
½ ounce ancho chile liqueur
½ ounce tepache (see page 88)
½ ounce banana liqueur
¾ ounce spiced honey syrup (see page 175)
¼ ounce pineapple juice
¾ ounce fresh lime juice
2 dashes Angostura bitters

Garnish:
Banana leaf
Lime wheel, scored
Whole nutmeg, grated

Combine all but bitters in a shaker with ice. Shake and pour into a skull or tall Tiki mug lined with a banana leaf. Top with pebbled ice and float bitters on top. Garnish with a scored lime wheel and freshly grated nutmeg.

ABEILLE

The flavors of France and the French Antilles—absinthe, Chartreuse, and infused rhum agricoles—come together, creating layers of vegetal and herbal notes tempered by vanilla and guava, popular ingredients in Martinique-style rum punches. Sous vide infusions look more inolved than they truly are, and once mastered they are a quick and surprisingly simple way to accomplish what would take literal months via traditional infusion methods. Since the ingredients are never directly exposed to the heat in a sous vide, even fresh flavors remain bright and potent. Adding a liqueur, such as Tempus Fugit Crème de Cacao, in place of the syrup lets you skip the infusion step, but the result is actually a sweeter, less intense cocktail.

Recommended spirits:
Damoiseau 110 Proof Rhum Agricole Blanc
St. George Absinthe Verte

1½ ounces sous vide rhum arrangé épices (recipe follows)
½ ounce yellow Chartreuse
¼ ounce absinthe
½ ounce guava puree
½ ounce vanilla syrup (see page 175)
¾ ounce fresh lime juice
2 dashes Angostura bitters

Garnish:
Edible flower
Lime shell, scored

Combine all but bitters in a shaker with cubed ice. Shake and strain into a Collins glass over ice. Top with pebbled ice and float bitters on top. Garnish with an edible flower and a scored lime shell.

Sous Vide Rhum Arrangé Épices: Combine 1 split vanilla bean, 2 to 3 cinnamon sticks, and ¼ cup fresh ginger coins (sliced from 1 piece of unpeeled ginger) with 25⅓ ounces (750 milliliters) rhum agricole blanc in a food-grade vacuum bag and seal tightly. Try to get all the air out of the bag before sealing. Place the bag in a large saucepan or stock pot, clip the sous vide wand to the side, and fill the pot with water until both bag and wand are fully submerged—you want to leave about 2 inches of clearance above the water line, so don't overfill.

Following your sous vide wand's instructions, set at 140°F for 2 hours—experiment with longer infusion times for more pronounced flavor, if desired. Remove the vacuum bag from the water bath and let cool. Strain the infused rhum through cheesecloth, discarding solids. Transfer to a clean, airtight bottle and store indefinitely in a cool place away from direct sunlight.

LEATHERBOUND

Consider this a dark, savory iced Mexican coffee, in which flavors of herbs, spice, and bitter cocoa are stacked one on top of another. Guinness brings nutty caramel notes and heft and mouthfeel aimed at pleasing those who enjoy a little cream in their coffee.

Recommended spirits:
Paranubes Rum
Marie Brizard Orange Curaçao
St. George Absinthe Verte

2 ounces anise-infused aguardiente (see page 160)
¼ ounce orange Curaçao
¼ ounce Amargo-Vallet Angostura
¼ ounce absinthe
½ ounce coffee syrup (see page 176)
Dark stout, preferably Guinness

Garnish:
Star anise, toasted

Combine all but the stout in a mixing glass with ice and stir briefly to chill, about 10 seconds. Strain into a chilled pilsner glass over pebbled ice. Top with the stout and garnish with a toasted star anise.

ONE LOVE

Shape-shifting is the name of the game here. Charged with creating a vodka cocktail for an event, I faced a dilemma: Vodka is not about flavor unless it's artificially added. I looked for ways to jazz it up—at that time, I was obsessed with fat-washing and decided to apply this technique to vodka. I did not anticipate what ensued—an aromatic, creamy, lush, and inexplicably dry drink. Coconut and cacao come together to cover all of these dimensions, softened by pineapple, which, as an emulsifier, brings a silkiness to the mouthfeel that recalls coconut milk without the heft. Seek this out if you are in the mood for a dry, complex take on the Piña Colada.

Recommended spirits:
Sobieski Estate Vodka
Tempus Fugit Crème de Cacao

2 ounces coconut oil–washed vodka (recipe follows)
½ ounce crème de cacao
1 ounce honey syrup (see page 175)
½ ounce pineapple juice
¾ ounce fresh lime juice

Garnish:
Pineapple wedge
Pineapple spear

Combine all in a shaker with cubed ice. Shake and strain into a Collins glass over ice. Top with pebbled ice and garnish with a pineapple wedge and spear.

Coconut Oil–Washed Vodka: Combine 12 ounces unrefined coconut oil (unrefined is necessary for the desired effect; refined coconut oil is odorless and flavorless) with 34 ounces (1 liter) vodka in a glass or nonporous, nonreactive container with a lid. Shake to mix, then let steep at room temperature for 4 to 6 hours. Transfer to the freezer for at least 4 hours or overnight to let the oil solidify.

Remove from the freezer, then discard the solidified oil and skim off any remaining solids. Double strain the vodka through cheesecloth before using. The coconut oil–washed vodka will keep indefinitely in an airtight container in the refrigerator.

TIGER'S MILK

Aromatic and creamy coconut is given additional heft and body by mellow but potent higher-proof rye whiskey, which carries vanilla, crème brûlée, and black pepper notes. Bright and punchy tamarind pairs nicely with lemon. Coffee brings a touch of dry tannin into the mix, grounding the drink with earthy notes that introduce a hint of savory. Follow the same coconut oil–washing technique as for the bourbon in the Tigershark (see page 61), but notice the drier and spicier flavors it brings out here in the rye.

Recommended spirits:
Rittenhouse Rye Whiskey 100 proof Bottled In Bond
Tamworth Distilling Von Humboldt's Natur Wasser Tamarind Cordial

2 ounces coconut oil–washed rye whiskey (see page 61)
½ ounce tamarind liqueur
½ ounce coffee syrup (see page 176)
1 ounce coconut cream
¾ ounce fresh lemon juice

Garnish:
Cinnamon stick, grated
Cocoa powder

Combine all in a shaker with pebbled ice. Flash blend with a stand or wand mixer for 10 to 15 seconds, then pour into a young coconut shell set in a coconut husk (see page 180), single-serve Tiki bowl, or bamboo mug wrapped with a banana leaf. Garnish with grated cinnamon and a dusting of cocoa powder.

RIVER STYX

Karen Fu, The Studio at the Freehand New York
Naming this cocktail after the boundary river of the Underworld, Karen Fu was inspired
by the Saturn, the classic Tiki cocktail from 1967 featuring passion fruit, lemon,
falernum, orgeat, and dry gin. In Karen's version, the hot infusion of habanero in
the tequila is tempered by bright caraway notes in the aquavit and the burnt funk of
Jamaican rum. The pale, sweet sherry bridges the spirits, citrus, and sugar.

Recommended spirits:
Cimmarón Blanco Tequila
Krogstad Aquavit
Hamilton Jamaican Pot Still Black Rum
Lustau East India Solera Sherry

1 ounce habanero-infused tequila (recipe follows)
½ ounce aquavit
½ ounce pot still Jamaican rum
½ ounce pale cream sherry
¾ ounce passion fruit puree
¾ ounce cinnamon syrup (see page 176)
¾ ounce fresh lemon juice

Garnish:
Pink peppercorns, crushed
Paper umbrella

Combine all in a shaker with cubed ice. Shake and strain into a snifter glass over crushed ice.
Garnish with freshly crushed pink peppercorns and serve with a paper umbrella.

Habanero-Infused Tequila: Stem and thinly slice 4 habanero peppers crosswise. Keep in mind
that the main source of heat is the seeds, so keep or remove seeds according to your preference.
Combine sliced habaneros with 34 ounces (1 liter) blanco tequila in a glass or nonporous,
nonreactive container. Gently agitate to mix and let infuse at room temperature for up to
15 minutes, tasting after 10 minutes to check heat level.

Strain and discard the solids, especially the seeds (any left in will continue to add heat). Return
infused tequila to original bottle (consider adding a label so you don't forget that it's been infused)
or store in an airtight container.

RUM FIREWALKER

Jason Alexander, Tacoma Cabana and Devil's Reef, Tacoma, Washington
This recipe, created by Jason Alexander, comes courtesy of Nick Feris, founder of The Rum Collective.

Recommended spirit:
Hampden Estate Rum Fire Overproof

3 ounces overproof Jamaican rum
1 ounce Campari
1 ounce cinnamon syrup (see page 176)
1 ounce fresh lime juice

Garnish:
Mint sprig
Edible flower

Combine all in a shaker with ice. Shake to chill, then pour into a Collins glass over cubed ice. Garnish with a mint sprig and an edible flower.

THE S.O.S. MAI TAI

Ean Bancroft, S.O.S. Tiki Bar, Atlanta, Georgia
I do my best to refrain from showing favoritism, but I won't here. My first visit to
S.O.S. remains one of my favorite experiences to date. The entire crew gave top-notch
hospitality, and Ean, who is a trained chef turned barman, welcomed me behind the bar
to trade tips on the best way to make a Daiquiri and Ti' Punch. Meanwhile, I'd embraced
the Mai Tai early on as one of my flagship cocktails at my first rum-focused bar project.
It follows that after keeping one on the menu for five years running, I am not easily
impressed by various iterations floating around out there. Ean's, however, does not fail
to deliver. The flaming garnish is a fun spectacle, but also requires some caution and
careful steps (see Note).

Recommended spirits:
Hamilton Jamaican Pot Still Black Rum
La Favorite Coeur de Canne Rhum Agricole Blanc
Rhum Clément Créole Shrubb

1½ ounces pot still Jamaican rum
½ ounce rhum agricole blanc
½ ounce orange Curaçao
¾ ounce orgeat (see page 176)
¾ ounce fresh lime juice

Garnish:
Flaming lime shell (see page 182)

Combine all ingredients in a shaker and add a handful of ice. Shake vigorously and pour all
contents into a Collins glass and top with fresh pebbled ice. Garnish with a flaming lime shell.

Note: For added excitement, sprinkle ground cinnamon from a shaker or sifter over the flame to
create impressive campfire-like sparks. Be mindful of your surroundings, as the sparks can jump
as much as 18 to 24 inches above the drink. Use common safety measures that come into play
when working with open flame—tie any loose hair back, roll up your sleeves, and make sure
you're in a well-ventilated area with a fire extinguisher handy.

Seven

FROZEN AND BLENDED

These are the drinks that made Tiki infamous, and with good reason. When done right, they are transcendently delicious; but when not, you risk a disastrously sweet or pitifully watery cocktail, which is no one's idea of a good time. Meanwhile, they tend to involve a fair number of ingredients, so it's not easy just to let it go when things go less than stellar here. With that in mind, Karen Jarman, a veteran of Sasha Petraske establishments and opening staff at the iconic and now-closed Tiki bar PKNY, offers these guidelines for successful drink blending: Add crushed or small pieces of ice to the blender so that there is a bit of dry ice peeking above the level of the liquid, then blend. The perfect consistency should be a little thicker than a smoothie so that you have to swirl the blender pitcher a little to pour into a glass.

As in the previous chapters, the following recipes are single serves. It is possible to double or even triple the quantities. However, since these drinks require the extra step of blending, I don't recommend scaling up more than this in a single blender—the final balance and texture could easily veer off base. If you are entertaining a group with frozen drinks, I suggest premixing batches of the nonalcoholic components ahead of time—a 1-liter bottle will yield 4 to 6 serves depending on the drink. Then, when ready to make drinks, measure out the required portion of the pre-mixed ingredients, then simply add the right proportion of spirits. Cocktails based on the Daiquiri—the Parasol (see page 39), the Royal Bermuda Yacht Club (see page 27), and Isle of Martinique (see page 34)—are all great options.

PLANTEUR AU VANILLE

In this mash-up of two iconic Tiki classics, the Piña Colada and the Planteur, the former's bone-dry Spanish-style rum is replaced by a fuller-flavored rhum agricole that gets extra dimension from an infusion of vanilla. The sous vide method results in a cleaner, brighter vanilla flavor than a traditional maceration method, and in a fraction of the time—the traditional way of preparing rhum arrangé can take anywhere from 6 to 12 months. Toasted coconut adds another layer of depth enhanced by banana liqueur.

Recommended spirits:
Damoiseau 110 Proof Rhum Agricole Blanc
Tempus Fugit Crème de Banane

2 ounces sous vide vanilla–infused rhum agricole (recipe follows)
1 ounce banana liqueur
½ ounce toasted coconut syrup (see page 175)
1 ounce guava puree
½ ounce fresh lime juice

Garnish:
Cinnamon stick, grated
Dehydrated pineapple chip

Combine all in a blender with scant ice. Blend on high speed for 10 to 15 seconds. (If blending batches, add about 5 more seconds per additional serve.) Pour into a chilled Collins glass. Garnish with grated cinnamon and a dehydrated pineapple chip.

Sous Vide Vanilla–Infused Rhum Agricole: Combine 1 split vanilla bean and 3 to 4 whole star anise with 34 ounces (1 liter) rhum agricole in a food-grade vacuum bag. Seal tightly, trying to get all the air out of the bag before sealing. Place the bag in a large saucepan or stock pot, clip the sous vide wand to the side, and fill the pot with water until both bag and wand are fully submerged— you want to leave about 2 inches of clearance above the water line, so don't overfill.

Following your sous vide wand's instructions, set at 140°F for 2 hours—experiment with longer infusion times for more pronounced flavor, if desired. Remove the vacuum bag from the water bath and let cool. Strain the infused rhum through cheesecloth, discarding solids. Transfer to a clean, airtight bottle and store indefinitely in a cool place away from direct sunlight.

FLIGHT OF THE ALBATROSS

Dry herbal notes come together to anchor this play on a boozy milkshake. Red rice's floral and nutty character is complemented by fragrant almonds in the horchata, while cinnamon adds piquant spice. The result is a creamy, rich drink with subtle dark cocoa notes that add a touch of sweetness.

Recommended spirit:
Paranubes Rum

2 ounces anise-infused aguardiente (see page 60)
½ ounce cinnamon syrup (see page 176)
½ ounce red rice horchata (see page 105)
½ ounce fresh lime juice

Garnish:
Cinnamon stick, grated
Lime, zested

Combine all in a blender with scant ice. Blend for 10 seconds. Pour into a Collins glass and garnish with grated cinnamon and freshly grated lime zest.

BIRDMAN

Mezcal's rough edges are smoothed out by creamy, buttery avocado, and papaya gives the slightly herbaceous oil a further lift. Amaro di Angostura—a rum-based liqueur made with the proprietary blend of barks and herbs found in the iconic bitters of the same name—brings a touch of cocoa and gentle spice. Chile liqueur adds a pop of acidity and lends a long, dry note to the finish.

Recommended spirits:
Del Maguey Vida Mezcal
Ancho Reyes Ancho Chile Liqueur

1½ ounces avocado oil–washed mezcal (recipe follows)
1 ounce Amaro di Angostura
¼ ounce chile liqueur
1 ounce papaya puree
½ ounce fresh lime juice

Garnish:
Pineapple leaves

Combine all in a blender with scant ice. Blend on high speed for 10 to 15 seconds. Pour into a chilled Collins glass. Garnish with 2 pineapple leaves.

Avocado Oil–Washed Mezcal: Combine 12 ounces avocado oil (more than for a typical fat-wash due to the intensity of the flavors in the spirit) and 34 ounces (1 liter) mezcal in a glass or nonporous, nonreactive container, and let steep at room temperature for 4 to 6 hours. Transfer to the freezer for another 8 hours or overnight to allow the oil solidify.

Remove the container from the freezer. Remove and discard the solidified oil and skim off any remaining solids, then double strain the infused mezcal through cheesecloth before using. Transfer to a clean bottle and store indefinitely in a cool place away from direct sunlight.

ETERNAL MYSTERY BLOSSOM

Pisco, a grape-based spirit that is the national beverage of Peru (and also enjoyed in Bolivia and Chile), can be as herbaceous as it is floral. When paired with an overproof Jamaican rum, the floral aromas become even more pronounced, brought into further high relief by the round fruit flavors of mango. Yuzu fans out the flavor profile with bright citrus notes that blossom on the finish.

Recommended spirits:

Macchu Pisco
Hampden Estate Rum Fire Overproof
Marie Brizard Yuzu Liqueur

1 ounce pisco
1 ounce overproof Jamaican rum
¼ ounce yuzu liqueur
½ ounce mango puree
½ ounce fresh lime juice

Garnish:
Lime, zested

Combine all in a blender with scant pebbled ice. Flash blend on high speed for 10 seconds. Pour into a chilled hurricane glass and garnish with freshly grated lime zest.

TAMARINDITA

A favorite dessert ingredient in Asian and Latin American cuisines, tamarind is, at turns, acidic, earthy, and slightly sweet; in drinks, it is delightfully bright, piquant, and zippy. Banana and Panamanian rum—known for its balance of dry, aromatic fruit and buttery toffee notes—add layers of roundness to the palate, while the amari bring bitter cacao nibs and an element of savory to tie it all together.

Recommended spirit:
Ron Abuelo 7-Year Añejo Rum

2 ounces aged rum
½ ounce Cynar
1 ounce tamarind puree
1 ounce banana milk (recipe follows)
¼ ounce fernet

Garnish:
Cinnamon stick, grated

Combine all but fernet in a blender with ice. Flash blend for 15 seconds and strain into a rocks glass over pebbled ice. Top with Fernet and garnish with freshly grated cinnamon.

Banana Milk: Peel 1 ripe banana, then cut into chunks and freeze until solid. Combine frozen banana, 1 cup water, ½ teaspoon vanilla extract, 1 teaspoon honey or syrup sweetener, 1 teaspoon cocoa powder, ¼ teaspoon cinnamon, and ¼ teaspoon freshly grated nutmeg in a blender and puree on high speed until smooth, adding water if needed. Banana milk is best used right away, but will keep in the refrigerator for up to 2 days (some discoloration may occur). You can extend that by a couple of days by adding 1 ounce of high-strength spirit to the mix—a 151-proof aged rum is delicious.

BAMBOO TRAIL

Shochu, distilled from barley in a process similar to that used to make sake from polishing rice, can exhibit flavors ranging from floral to fruity to earthy. Calpico, a creamy milk-based beverage that is superpopular in Japan, pairs with the mild, nutty sweetness of orgeat. Passion fruit adds a tart curveball element, and the result is a light, easy-drinking version of an orange Push Pop, minus the cloying sweetness, brightened by floral notes.

Recommended spirits:
Iichiko Mugi Shochu
Lustau Dry Amontillado "Los Arcos" Solera Reserva Sherry

2 ounces shochu
1 ounce amontillado sherry
1 ounce Calpico concentrate
½ ounce orgeat (see page 176)
½ ounce passion fruit juice
¾ ounce fresh lime juice

Garnish:
Lime, zested
Edible flower

Combine all in a blender with pebbled ice. Flash blend for 10 seconds and pour into a chilled bamboo glass. Garnish with freshly grated lime zest and an edible flower.

ISLA DE BOTANICA

Avocado oil–washed cachaça takes the place of coconut cream in this more fruit-forward version of the Piña Colada, while mango brings a mild hint of savory. Meanwhile, passion fruit–honey syrup does double duty, mimicking the bright, clean flavor of pineapple as well as adding a level of viscosity.

Recommended Spirit:
Yaguara Cachaça Ouro

2 ounces avocado oil–washed cachaça (recipe follows)
¾ ounce passion fruit–honey syrup (see page 175)
½ ounce mango puree
¾ ounce fresh lime juice

Garnish:
Edible flower

Combine all in a blender with scant ice, and flash blend for 15 seconds. Pour into a chilled coupe glass and garnish with an edible flower.

Avocado Oil–Washed Cachaça: Combine 6 ounces avocado oil and 25⅓ ounces (750 milliliters) cachaça in a glass or nonporous, nonreactive container, and let steep at room temperature for 6 hours. Transfer the container to the freezer for another 8 hours to allow the oil to solidify.

Remove the container from the freezer. Remove and discard the solidified oil and skim off any remaining solids, then double strain the cachaça through cheesecloth before using. In an airtight container, the avocado oil–washed cachaça will keep indefinitely in the refrigerator.

SHOCHULADA

A cornucopia of lush and aromatic fruits are layered one on top of another here—lychee's delicate floral notes pair up with those in the coconut and shochu, which also share savory and nutty flavors. Spice and tangy citrus come into the picture with both falernum and Don's Mix, an iconic blend of cinnamon syrup and grapefruit juice. The result is a pleasant and smooth cocktail perfectly suited to leisurely, laid-back day drinking.

Recommended spirit:
Iichiko Mugi Shochu

2 ounces coconut oil–washed shochu (recipe follows)
1 ounce Don's Mix (see page 176)
½ ounce falernum (see page 171)
½ ounce lychee juice
¾ ounce fresh lime juice

Garnish:
Lime, zested

Combine all in a blender with pebbled ice. Blend for 10 seconds. Pour into a chilled snifter. Garnish with freshly grated lime zest.

Coconut Oil–Washed Shochu: Combine 6 ounces unrefined coconut oil (unrefined is necessary for the desired effect; refined coconut oil is odorless and flavorless) with 23½ ounces (700 milliliters) of shochu in a glass or nonporous, nonreactive container with a lid. Shake to mix, then let steep at room temperature for 4-6 hours. Transfer to the freezer for at least 4 hours or overnight to allow the oil solidify.

Remove from the freezer, then discard the solidified oil and skim off any remaining solids. Doublestrain the shochu through cheesecloth before using. The coconut oil–washed shochu will keep indefinitely in an airtight container in the refrigerator (or freezer).

ENCANTAMENTO

Soursop is one of my favorite tropical fruit juices for its unexpected nuance and complexity. Commonly found in Caribbean markets, you can source it online—the Rubicon, Goya, or Le Fe brands are all trusted by Tiki mixologits. Slightly milky in appearance, it is floral and fruity with a long, dry finish, described as a cross between a pineapple and a pear. Here, it serves as a unifying thread for the range of flavors found in the other ingredients. Bright, piquant cinnamon; floral, slightly nutty coconut; and the soft, restrained vegetal notes of tequila are all softened by the avocado oil.

Recommended spirit:
Tequila Tromba Reposado

2 ounces avocado oil–washed tequila (recipe follows)
½ ounce toasted coconut syrup (see page 175)
½ ounce cinnamon syrup (see page 176)
1 ounce soursop juice
¾ ounce fresh lime juice

Garnish:
Banana leaf
Dehydrated blood orange wheel
Lime, zested

Combine all in a blender with light ice and flash blend for 15 seconds. Pour into a chilled rocks glass lined with a banana leaf. Garnish with a dehydrated blood orange wheel and freshly grated lime zest.

Avocado Oil–Washed Tequila: Combine 6 ounces avocado oil and 25⅓ ounces (750 milliliters) reposado tequila in a glass or nonporous, nonreactive container, and let steep at room temperature for 6 hours. Transfer the container to the freezer for another 8 hours or overnight to allow the oil to solidify.

Remove the container from the freezer. Remove and discard the solidified oil and skim off any remaining solids, then double strain the tequila through cheesecloth before using. Transfer to a clean bottle and store indefinitely in a cool place away from direct sunlight.

WINDFALL

Karen Jarman, Brand Manager, Yola Mezcal, New York
This delicious, fresh cocktail comes from a friend, spirits consultant Karen Jarman: "My bartending life began after a flash of intuition and a serendipitous meeting with one of the owners [of Dutch Kills] at a charity food event. At the late PKNY [formerly Painkiller] on Essex Street, I discovered the happiness frozen drinks could bring to a crowd and how fantastic they are when made well with fresh ingredients. This drink is my take on that style, giving nontropical ingredients a tropical vibe through the form. With its hints of a Piña Colada, you could call this 'Northeast Tiki' or something like that."

Recommended spirits:
Yola 1971 Mezcal
Sho Chiku Bai Nigori Sake

1 ounce mezcal espadín
1½ ounce nigori sake
1 ounce honey syrup (see page 175)
1 section roasted pear (recipe follows)
¼ ounce fresh lemon juice
Pinch fresh lemon zest
¼ ounce Varnelli Amaro Sibilla

Garnish:
Rosemary sprig
Edible flower

In a blender, combine mezcal, sake, honey syrup, pear, lemon juice, and lemon zest. Add just enough crushed or small pieces of ice so that a small amount of ice peeks above the level of the liquid. Blend on high speed for 15 to 20 seconds. Pour into a chilled glass and float the amaro around the rim. Garnish with a fresh rosemary sprig or an edible flower.

Roasted Pear: Preheat oven to 350ºF and line a baking sheet with parchment paper. Peel and core 1 ripe pear (I prefer Anjou or Bosc, but try your favorite), then halve and slice each half into 3 wedges for 6 sections total. Transfer the pear wedges to the baking sheet, drizzle with olive oil, and roast in the oven for 45 minutes, until tender. Let cool.

HIGH TIDE

Infusing bourbon with toasted banana adds pleasant spiciness and, depending on the style you choose, it can render the spirit rounder and creamier or highlight the sharp charred-wood notes from the barrel. No matter which way you decide to go with this one, the pineapple balances it with the addition of soft fruit, and the allspice dram's spicy, woody notes bring it full circle.

Recommended spirits:
Old Grand-Dad 114 Proof Bourbon
St. Elizabeth Allspice Dram

2 ounces toasted banana chip–infused bourbon (recipe follows)
¼ ounce allspice dram
½ ounce spiced syrup (see page 176)
½ ounce pineapple juice
¾ ounce fresh lime juice

Garnish:
Pineapple chip
Pineapple spear
Cinnamon stick, grated

Combine all in a blender with ice, then blend on high speed for 15 to 20 seconds. Pour into a chilled Collins or Pearl Diver glass (see page 180) and garnish with a pineapple chip, pineapple spear, and freshly grated cinnamon.

Toasted Banana Chip–Infused Bourbon: In a saucepan over medium-low heat, toast ¼ cup banana chips until slightly browned and fragrant. Combine toasted banana chips with 16 ounces (475 milliliters) of bourbon in a covered glass or nonporous, nonreactive container and let steep at room temperature for 24 hours. Strain off the bourbon and discard the toasted banana chips. Store in the refrigerator for up to 4 weeks.

Eight

COMMUNAL DRINKS

The idea behind a big, fun punch is that it makes the host's job easier and more manageable, especially with a large group to entertain. Rather than making single-serve cocktails to order—and finding oneself stuck behind the bar the whole time—communal and self-serve drinks free the host to enjoy the party. These recipes also benefit from time for the flavors to marry and mellow, so mix up one or more batches a day or two in advance.

Many cocktail recipes from preceding chapters adapt well to scaling up into communal drinks, but wise hosts will stick to those with five or fewer ingredients. One's mastery of the multiplication tables aside, they are simply that much easier to keep the flavors in balance. The more components included in the punch, the greater the opportunity for a mistake in measuring or mixing, throwing off the drink and wasting ingredients in the process.

When it comes to garnish, now is the time to have fun and be over-the-top and extravagant. Be they fresh, frozen, or dehydrated, citrus wheels—lemon, lime, orange, blood orange—are a great way to add color and subtle flavor to bowls or punches. Edible flowers add an elegant, exotic element floating in a punch. Fresh cinnamon or nutmeg adds an aromatic finishing touch when grated over fuller-bodied punches. For a refreshing herbal element for punches with agricole rums or piscos, offer an atomizer or mister filled with absinthe for guests to spritz over each serving.

See page 173 for tips on keeping communal drinks cold without unwanted dilution.

BUCCANEER'S BOUNTY

Dark, rich, and earthy, this bowl is an excellent choice for fall. Warm spice notes from the rum and cinnamon get a bit of heft from oaky, peppery rye. Soursop, which strikes an uncommon balance between fruity and dry, brings in pleasant pineapple and pear flavors. Finally, Angostura bitters, rather like seasoning, amplify all of these elements and bring a bright punchiness to the proceedings.

Recommended spirits:
Hamilton 86 Demerara Rum
Rittenhouse 100 Proof Bottled In Bond Rye Whiskey

250 milliliters (8½ ounces) spiced Guyana rum
125 milliliters (4¼ ounces) rye whiskey
100 milliliters (3⅓ ounces) cinnamon syrup (see page 176)
125 milliliters (4¼ ounces) soursop juice
125 milliliters (4¼ ounces) fresh lime juice
50 milliliters (1½ ounces) Angostura bitters

Garnish:
Citrus wheels
Edible flowers

Combine all ingredients in a nonreactive container and stir to mix. Decant over ice into a Tiki bowl or serving vessel of your choice. Serve with straws and garnish with citrus wheels and edible flowers.

PARAISO ETERNO

The floral aromas of anise give a gentle lift to those found in the coconut, while vanilla complements the herbal and earthy notes and adds a touch of creaminess. Green chile brings it all full circle, touching on all of these while adding a bit of bite to the drink and lengthening its slightly dry finish.

Recommended spirits:
Diplomatíco Planas
Ancho Reyes Verde Chile Poblano Liqueur

250 milliliters (8½ ounces) anise-infused aged white rum (recipe follows)
50 milliliters (1½ ounces) green chile liqueur
125 milliliters (4¼ ounces) vanilla syrup (see page 175)
100 milliliters (3⅓ ounces) coconut water
180 milliliters (6 ounces) fresh lime juice

Garnish:
Citrus wheels
Edible flowers

Combine all ingredients in a nonreactive container and stir to mix. Decant over ice into a Tiki bowl or serving vessel of your choice. Serve with straws and garnish with citrus wheels and edible flowers.

Anise-Infused Aged White Rum: Combine 2 tablespoons whole anise seeds with 34 ounces (1 liter) aged white rum in a glass or nonporous, nonreactive container. Gently mix, then let steep at room temperature for 24 hours. Fine strain and discard the seeds before use. Decant the infused rum into a clean bottle and store indefinitely in a cool place away from direct sunlight.

OLD ROGUE

Three spirits—funky Jamaican rum; smooth, sweet Cognac; and earthy, slightly rough Batavia arrack—join floral pineapple, vegetal green tea, and orange Curaçao, a classic citrus liqueur made from bitter orange peels. Big bodied but buoyed by bright fruit and grounded by spice, this recipe covers all the defining elements of the eighteenth-century punches that put sugarcane spirits and layered, multi-ingredient drinks on the map.

Recommended spirits:
Hamilton Jamaican Pot Still Black Rum
Pierre Ferrand 1840 Original Formula Cognac
Batavia Arrack van Oosten
Marie Brizard Orange Curaçao

250 milliliters (8½ ounces) pot still Jamaican rum
100 milliliters (3⅓ ounces) Cognac
50 milliliters (1½ ounces) Batavia arrack
50 milliliters (1½ ounces) orange Curaçao
125 milliliters (4¼ ounces) green tea syrup (see page 176)
50 milliliters (1½ ounces) pineapple juice
100 milliliters (3⅓ ounces) fresh lemon juice

Garnish:
Citrus wheels
Edible flowers

Combine all ingredients in a nonreactive container and stir to mix. Decant over ice into a Tiki bowl or serving vessel of your choice. Serve with straws and garnish with citrus wheels and edible flowers.

CAPTAIN'S QUARTERS

Navy Grog (see page 32)—rum, sugar, and lime—gets a touch of class with the addition of an aged rhum agricole. Its time in a barrel tempers and mellows the concentrated fruit and floral aromas, which get an additional layer of depth and sophistication by the rich tannins present in black tea. For tea lovers out there, I suggest experimenting with other dark, sturdy brews, especially those with a faint floral dimension, such as Assam and Keemun.

Recommended spirits:
Pusser's Gunpowder Proof British Navy Rum
Navy Rum Bend (see page 169)
La Favorite Coeur d'Ambre Rhum Agricole

250 milliliters (8½ ounces) Navy-style rum
100 milliliters (3⅓ ounces) rhum agricole ambre
125 milliliters (4¼ ounces) Demerara syrup (see page 175)
125 milliliters (4¼ ounces) fresh lime juice
50 milliliters (1½ ounces) brewed Ceylon tea

Garnish:
Citrus wheels
Edible flowers

Combine all ingredients in a nonreactive container and stir to mix. Decant over ice into a Tiki bowl or serving vessel of your choice. Serve with straws and garnish with citrus wheels and edible flowers.

ARCHIPELAGO

Calvados, brandy made from apples and renowned for its dry and fruity character, comes together with the malty, earthen spice of Batavia arrack, a sort of predecessor of rum from the island of Java, made from fermented red rice and molasses or sugarcane. Pear liqueur and ginger syrup add delicious baking-spice notes and a pleasant silkiness to temper the acidity that sparkles and shines throughout.

Recommended spirits:
Batavia Arrack van Oosten
Lemorton Pommeau de Normandie
Rothman & Winter Orchard Pear Liqueur

250 milliliters (8½ ounces) aged Batavia arrack
100 milliliters (3⅓ ounces) Calvados
50 milliliters (1½ ounces) pear liqueur
125 milliliters (4¼ ounces) ginger syrup (see page 176)
100 milliliters (3⅓ ounces) fresh lemon juice

Garnish:
Citrus wheels
Edible flowers

Combine all ingredients in a nonreactive container and stir to mix. Decant over ice into a Tiki bowl or serving vessel of your choice. Serve with straws and garnish with citrus wheels and edible flowers.

Many Tiki bowls include a minibowl for a flame garnish, safely away from the body of the drink. Top with a scant amount of 151-proof rum (see page 168) or soak a sugar cube, and carefully ignite before serving. Always blow out the flame before drinking and take all appropriate cautions when working with open flame (see page 182).

KOOPMAN

The addition of Earl Grey tea and tangerine juice amplify and accent the aromatic and botanical aspects of both the arrack and the gin, which derive their flavor profiles from citrus, flowers, and botanicals. I chose a barrel-aged expression, fuller bodied and slightly malty, to evoke the genevers that enjoyed a similar popularity as Batavia arrack in the eighteenth century. Spicy, dry, and aromatic, I enjoy this in the fall or winter as a perfect accompaniment to a festive holiday gathering.

Recommended spirits:
Captive Spirits Bourbon Barreled Big Gin
Batavia Arrack van Oosten

500 milliliters (17 ounces) barrel-aged gin
250 milliliters (8½ ounces) Batavia arrack
250 milliliters (8½ ounces) lemongrass syrup (see page 176)
500 milliliters (17 ounces) tangerine juice
250 milliliters (8½ ounces) fresh lime juice
250 milliliters (8½ ounces) brewed Earl Grey tea

Garnish:
Citrus wedges
Citrus wheels
Whole nutmeg, grated

Combine all ingredients and stir to mix. Keep at least 4 hours or up to overnight in a covered container in the refrigerator. Stir before serving. If using a punch bowl, pour over a large block of ice to slow dilution. Garnish with citrus wedges, citrus wheels, and freshly grated nutmeg.

ANTILLES JEWEL

Enjoy this light take on a classic Barbados rum punch, in which the spicy notes in the rums are softened by creamy banana and earthy crème de cacao. Mildly nutty coconut water ties it all together, resulting in a refreshing, easy-drinking punch, perfect for an afternoon spent on deck listening to the waves.

Recommended spirits:

Mount Gay Black Barrel Rum
Hamilton 86 Demerara Rum
Tempus Fugit Crème de Banane
Giffard Crème de Cacao Blanc

500 milliliters (17 ounces) aged Barbados rum
250 milliliters (8½ ounces) aged Demerara rum
200 milliliters (6¾ ounces) banana liqueur
100 milliliters (3⅓ ounces) white crème de cacao
250 milliliters (8½ ounces) coconut water
350 milliliters (12 ounces) fresh lime juice

Garnish:
Citrus wheels
Edible flowers

Combine all ingredients and stir to mix. Keep at least 4 hours or up to overnight in a covered container in the refrigerator. Stir before serving. If utilizing a punch bowl, pour over a large block of ice to slow dilution. Garnish with citrus wheels and edible flowers.

TRADEWINDS

Citrus in a handful of guises—fresh squeezed, pureed, and in liqueur form—all come into play here to provide a bright note to rich Barbados rum complemented by a splash of funky Jamaican rum. If fresh blood orange juice is hard to find, The Perfect Puree of Napa Valley makes a good substitute.

Recommended spirits:
Hamilton Jamaica Pot Still Black Rum
Mount Gay Black Barrel Rum
Rhum Clément Créole Shrubb

500 milliliters (17 ounces) pot still Jamaican rum
250 milliliters (8½ ounces) aged Barbados rum
250 milliliters (8½ ounces) orange liqueur
200 milliliters (6¾ ounces) fresh lemon juice
100 milliliters (3⅓ ounces) blood orange juice
50 milliliters (1½ ounces) Angostura bitters

Garnish:
Dehydrated blood orange wheels

Combine all ingredients and stir to mix. Keep at least 4 hours or up to overnight in a covered container in the refrigerator. Stir before serving. If utilizing a punch bowl, pour over a large block of ice to slow dilution. Garnish with dehydrated blood orange wheels

PORT OF CALL

A spicy Navy-strength sipper, think of this as a fancy Grog (see page 13), spruced up by the addition of specialty ingredients and elevated to the status of a punch fit for officers. Batavia arrack intersects with and amplifies the other elements, its slightly funky notes working in tandem with the Jamaican rum. The arrack's floral quality brings extra sparkle to the tangerine juice and finds a companion in the flinty earthiness of the rum. Allspice dram brings up the rear, bringing additional spice and citrus notes and soft tannins that tie it all together.

Recommended spirits:
Plantation O.F.T.D. Rum
Batavia Arrack van Oosten
Hampden Estate Rum Fire Overproof
Hamilton Pimento Dram Liqueur

300 milliliters (10 ounces) Navy-strength rum
100 milliliters (3⅓ ounces) Batavia arrack
100 milliliters (3⅓ ounces) overproof Jamaican rum
75 milliliters (2½ ounces) allspice dram
200 milliliters (6¾ ounces) tangerine juice
300 milliliters (10 ounces) fresh lime juice
100 milliliters (3⅓ ounces) Angostura bitters

Garnish:
Lime, zested
Whole nutmeg, grated

Combine all ingredients and stir to mix. Keep at least 4 hours or up to overnight in a covered container in the refrigerator. Stir before serving. If utilizing a punch bowl, pour over a large block of ice to slow dilution. Garnish with freshly grated lime zest and freshly grated nutmeg.

RIOS DEL MIEL

Rich, creamy, and aromatic milk punches were all the rage in eighteenth-century drink culture and seem to be making a resounding comeback in today's craft cocktail bars. The ingredient list can be a touch daunting, and one may wonder what makes it all worth the trouble. I have one word for you: mouthfeel—a truly luscious and silky mouthfeel, to be exact. Clarification is the process through which solids are removed from the milk, leaving the whey and the fat, which impart a silky texture to the liquid. Carried out in part to create drinks that had a long shelf life in the age before refrigeration, this method of preparation also serves to unite all the ingredients into a seamless and delicious whole. The use of unaged cachaça adds brightness.

Recommended spirits:

Yaguara Cachaça Prata
BarSol Pisco
Marie Brizard Yuzu Liqueur

12 lemons
1 whole ripe pineapple, peeled, cored, and cut into 1-inch cubes
20 whole coriander seeds
3 whole cloves
1 cinnamon stick
1 star anise
2 cups sugar
250 milliliters (8½ ounces) freshly brewed Sencha tea, hot
237 milliliters (8 ounces) water, boiling
750 milliliters (25⅓ ounces) unaged cachaça
250 milliliters (8½ ounces) pisco
250 milliliters (8½ ounces) falernum (see page 171)
125 milliliters (4¼ ounces) yuzu liqueur
1 liter (34 ounces) whole milk

Garnish:
Edible flowers
Citrus wheels

With a peeler, remove peel from the lemons. Juice the peeled lemons and reserve the liquid; discard the squeezed-out solids. Combine the lemon peels, pineapple, spices, and sugar in a large bowl or nonporous, nonreactive container, and muddle. Pour in the brewed green tea and stir to mix. Add boiling water and immediately cover. Let sit overnight, then strain the mixture into a clean container, discarding the solid's. Add the cachaça, pisco, falernum, and yuzu liqueur.

Bring the milk to a boil. Add the hot milk and reserved lemon juice to the strained rum mixture—the milk will curdle and the solids will coagulate. Strain the liquid a little at a time through a fine mesh strainer or chinois lined with cheesecloth, replacing the cheesecloth if it becomes too thickly layered with milk solids.

Pour into a clean container, cover, and refrigerate again overnight to give any remaining milk solids time to settle. Strain again through a fine mesh strainer or chinois lined with cheesecloth, then transfer punch to a clean bottle and store in the refrigerator for up to 3 months.

Stir before serving. If utilizing a punch bowl, pour over a large block of ice to slow dilution.

Garnish with edible flowers and citrus wheels.

NO WOMAN NO CRY

Funky and earthy with dramatic floral notes, this punch balances the dry tannins of black tea and robust character of blackstrap rum with the bright acidity of pineapple juice.

Recommended spirits:
Hamilton Jamaica Pot Still Black Rum
Gosling's Black Seal 151 Rum

500 milliliters (17 ounces) pot still Jamaican rum
250 milliliters (8½ ounces) blackstrap rum
250 milliliters (8½ ounces) hibiscus syrup (see page 176)
100 milliliters (3⅓ ounces) pineapple juice
200 milliliters (6¾ ounces) fresh lime juice
100 milliliters (3⅓ ounces) brewed Ceylon tea
100 milliliters (3⅓ ounces) Angostura bitters
100 milliliters (3⅓ ounces) Peychaud's Bitters

Garnish:
Fresh and dehydrated citrus wheels

Combine all ingredients and stir to mix. Keep at least 4 hours or up to overnight in a covered container in the refrigerator. Stir before serving. If utilizing a punch bowl, pour over a large block of ice to slow dilution. Garnish with fresh and dehydrated citrus wheels.

ROYAL DOCK COOLER

Keep it simple and light with this play on the Daiquiri (see page 16), where the dial is turned all the way up with the addition of black tea and dried citrus.

Recommended spirit:
Hamilton Jamaican Pot Still Black Rum

750 milliliters (25⅓ ounces) pot still Jamaican rum
250 milliliters (8½ ounces) pineapple syrup (see page 176)
200 milliliters (6¾ ounces) grapefruit juice
50 milliliters (1½ ounces) brewed Earl Grey tea

Garnish:
Lime wheels

Combine all ingredients and stir to mix. Keep at least 4 hours or up to overnight in a covered container in the refrigerator. Stir before serving. If utilizing a punch bowl, pour over a large block of ice to slow dilution. Garnish with fresh lime wheels.

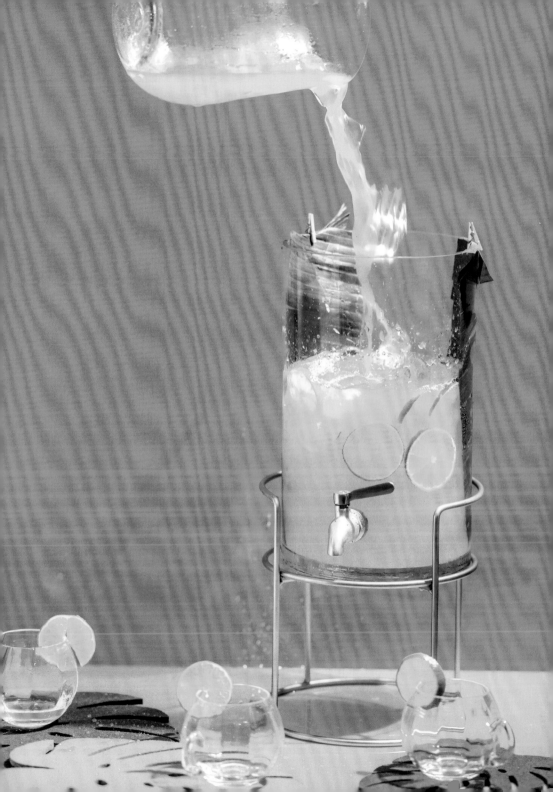

SCULLY COURT PUNCH

Bitters—essentially spices and herbs macerated in high-proof alcohol—are, in fact, a type of bottled cocktail, just sans sugar and citrus. Here, two bitters with the most profound ties to cocktail culture are lengthened and softened with the addition of a mellow bourbon—Mellow Corn is made from 90 percent corn and 10 percent rye and malted barley, then aged for at least two years. Ginger accents the spice notes of Angostura, while pineapple complements the sweetness of the Peychaud's.

Recommended spirit:
Mellow Corn Straight Corn Whiskey

500 milliliters (17 ounces) bourbon
250 milliliters (8½ ounces) ginger syrup (see page 176)
100 milliliters (3⅓ ounces) pineapple juice
200 milliliters (6¾ ounces) fresh lemon juice
125 milliliters (4¼ ounces) Angostura bitters
15 milliliters (½ ounce) Peychaud's Bitters

Garnish:
Lime wheels

Combine all ingredients and stir to mix. Keep at least 4 hours or up to overnight in a covered container in the refrigerator. Stir before serving. If utilizing a punch bowl, pour over a large block of ice to slow dilution. Garnish with lime wheels.

FOG CUTTER
The Brother Cleve Remix

I've played around with the Fog Cutter and revised its ingredients over the past few years, serving it in numerous bars and Tiki events. I like using a heavier Jamaican rum with the richer Cuban-style rum, abetted by the clean unaged brandy of Peru (I favor the Peruvian Quebranta grape varietal, though a pisco made from Italia brings in some citrus and pepper notes). East India Solera is an excellent cream-styled (sweetened) sherry, but I've also enjoyed playing around with amaro as a float, especially the higher-proof Cynar 70, for a different twist and a touch of herbaceousness. Here's my take on it.

Recommended spirits:
Santa Teresa 1796 Solera Rum
Hamilton Jamaican Pot Still Gold Rum
Macchu Pisco
Hayman's Royal Dock Navy Strength Gin
Tempus Fugit Crème de Noyaux
Lustau East India Solera Sherry

1 ounce Cuban-style rum
1 ounce pot still Jamaican rum
1 ounce Peruvian pisco
½ ounce Navy-strength gin
¼ oz crème de Noyaux
¼ ounce sesame syrup (recipe follows)
¾ ounce calamansi juice (or yuzu, if easier to find)
½ ounce sweetened oloroso sherry or Cynar

Garnish:
Mint sprig
Dehydrated blood orange wheel

Shake with ice and pour into a large snifter or Tiki mug. Float Lustau East India Solera Sherry or Cynar 70 on top. Garnish with fresh mint and a dehydrated blood orange wheel.

Sesame Syrup: Preheat oven to 350°F. Spread 2 cups raw sesame seeds on a baking sheet. Toast on the middle rack until lightly browned and fragrant, about 8 to 10 minutes. Combine toasted sesame seeds with 2 cups (475 milliliters) water in a small saucepan. Bring to a boil over medium-high heat, then simmer for 15 minutes, until reduced to 1 cup. Strain through a fine mesh strainer, discard the solids, and return the liquid to the same pan. Add 1 cup sugar and stir until dissolved. Transfer to an airtight container and keep in the refrigerator for up to 3 weeks.

MUSIC FOR TROPICAL COCKTAILS
Brother Cleve

When it comes to music to pair with tropical libations, my only rule of thumb is that the music should come from a place that has palm trees. That covers a lot of ground, of course. Looking at the wider Caribbean, each island has its own style of rum and its own style(s) of music, including Cuban-born sounds (often refined in Mexico) like the rhumba, mambo, cha-cha, guaracha, and danzon; Dominican merengue and bachata; Martinique's zouk; and the calypso and soca sounds of Trinidad, Tobago, Barbados, and Guyana. Brazilian cachaça blends smoothly with the mellow, jazzy bossa nova, as well as the adult-oriented-rock and samba-disco grooves of MPB (Música popular brasileira). These, in turn, were a direct influence on yacht rock, the soft rock/blue-eyed soul sound of the seventies and eighties (contemporary diggers such as Berlin's DJ Supermarkt, have unearthed many artists and songs that never hit the charts).

- *Skinny Dip With Don Tiki*, Don Tiki (Taboo Records, 2001)
- *Disc "O" Lypso* (Trans Air, 2003)
- *Hugo Mendez Presents: Tropical Funk Experience* (Nascente, 2009)
- *Jimmy Virani Is Beachcombing in Outer Space* (S Car Go, 2009)
- *New Sounds of Exotica*, The Waitiki 7 (Pass Out Records, 2010)
- *Third River Rangoon*, Mr. Ho's Orchestrotica (Exotica For Modern Living, 2011)
- *Bossa Nova and the Rise of Brazilian Music in the 1960s: Compiled by Gilles Peterson* (Soul Jazz Records, UK, 2011)
- *West Indies Funk*, 3 volumes (Trans Air, 2011)
- *Sofrito International Soundclash* (Strut, 2012)
- *Haiti Direct* (Strut, 2014)
- *Tropical Disco Hustle* (Cultures of Soul Records, 2015)
- *Brazilian Disco Boogie Sounds* (Favorite Recordings, France; 2014 & 2016)
- *Call of the Islands*, Ixtahuele (Subliminal Sounds, 2016)
- *The Ladies of Too Slow To Disco* (How Do You Are Records, Germany, 2014–17)

Exotica is a style of music originally popular in the early fifties and sixties that enjoyed a renewal of interest along with the resurgence of Tiki in the late nineties. Its first recording was Les Baxter and His Orchestra's *Ritual of the Savage (Le Sacre du Sauvage)*, a tone poem released in 1951. Baxter was heavily influenced by the works of artists like Stravinsky, Ravel, and Debussy, and mixed romantic orchestral music with "jungle" rhythms and percussion from Latin America, Africa, and Polynesia. In 1955, Hawaiian-based jazz musician Martin Denny took Baxter's music and arranged it for a jazz combo, adding bird calls, animal noises, and assorted jungle sounds produced by percussionist Augie Colón. They debuted at Don the Beachcomber in Honolulu's Hawaiian Village in 1955, and by 1958 had a top-ten hit with "Quiet Village."

Of course, plenty of classic and contemporary surf music can be added to the mix. Albums can be found in a wide variety of formats, including Internet radio and streaming, Mixcloud, SoundCloud, Bandcamp, YouTube, CD boxed sets, and both modern and vintage vinyl records. Not all have been reissued, and some original albums can go for upward of a few hundred dollars (although a few have been bootlegged).

- Arthur Lyman, *Taboo* (Hi-Fi Records, 1958)
- John McFarland, *Provocatif* (United Artists, 1959)
- The Outriggers, *Captivation* (Warner Bros., 1959)
- Phil Moore, *Polynesian Paradise* (Strand, 1959)
- Gene Rains, *Lotus Land* (Decca, 1960)
- Paul Conrad, *Exotic Paradise* (Mahalo, 1960)
- The Exciting Sounds of Milt Raskin, *Kapu* (Crown, 1959)
- The Surfmen, *The Sounds of Exotic Island* (Somerset, 1960)
- Stanley Black, *Exotic Percussion* (Decca, 1961)
- Alex Keack, *Surfers Paradise* (Crown, 1961)
- Ted Auletta, *Exotica* (Cameo, 1962)
- The Exotic Sounds of Rex Kona and His Mandarins, *Wild Orchids* (Columbia, 1964)
- *The Exotic Moods of Les Baxter*, 2-CD set (Capitol, 1996)
- *The Exotic Sounds of Martin Denny*, 2-CD set (Capitol, 1996)

SPIRITS

RUM AND CANE SPIRITS

Rum enjoys unique status in the world of spirits. Unlike the other major categories, there are no universally acknowledged guidelines as to what constitutes rum apart from a single criterion: It must be made from a sugar product, be it fresh cane juice, molasses, sugar crystals, or a combination of the three. Adding to its mystery, the flavor and texture of the finished rum often has more to do with its production and any aging or blending than where the sugarcane was grown—though terroir does come into play—making it both deliciously diverse and tricky to classify.

English-style rum, from former British colonies, including Barbados, Guyana, Trinidad and Tobago, St. Lucia, and Jamaica, dates back to the mid-seventeenth century. Distilled in pot and column stills like those used for single malt whiskey, this style is known for big, bold flavors. Long fermentation techniques give Jamaican **heavy pot still**, **high-ester rums** their famous funk (see page 78). **Demerara rum**, from the Guyanese river valley of the same name, is especially prized for heady floral and concentrated berry notes, smoke, and a chewy texture—qualities imparted by rich alluvial soils. These rums play well with others while retaining their unique character, especially in a cocktail that utilizes multiple rums (see page 80). By 1750, the British Navy had become the largest rum consumer in the world and sourced rums from multiple islands for an iconic custom blend of heavy pot still, high-proof spirit now known as **Navy-style rum** (see page 43).

Known for funky, vegetal, and grassy aromas, **French-style rums** (*rhums*) are produced on French Caribbean islands—including Martinique, Guadeloupe, and Marie-Galante—Réunion, and Mauritius. Rum made in this style from fresh-pressed cane juice is called *rhum agricole* (or agricole rum) to distinguish it from that made with molasses, *rhum industriel*. Hailed as one of the world's premiere sugarcane growing regions, Martinique's tropical heat, humidity, and fertile volcanic soil create a unique microclimate that shows in the bold and potent flavors of its rhum (see page 14). There are three broad categories of agricole rums—blanc, rested in stainless steel to allow the spirit to breathe and mellow before bottling; ambre, aged one to two years in wooden barrels; and vieux, aged five to eight years.

The Spanish colonies were late to take up large-scale rum production, due to resistance from Spanish wine and sherry makers to new competition. Nevertheless, Cuba, flat and ideal for growing sugarcane, soon distinguished itself as a producer of exceptional cane spirits. The Bacardi family's innovative use of yeast strains, high rectification in column stills, and charcoal filtration would eventually come to define **Spanish-style rum** (or *ron*). Crisp, dry, and without any funk or rough edges, these rums are best suited to light, easy cocktails (see page 30), with the Havana-born Daiquiri (see page 16) perhaps the ultimate, refreshing expression of the style. The Dominican Republic, Puerto Rico, Venezuela, and Nicaragua are also known for producing solid Spanish-style rums. Extra-aged styles, inspired by sherry production, often utilize the solera method, in which rums of different ages are blended for consistency and continuity of the house style.

Batavia arrack is a South Asian ancestor of rum made from a red rice starter fermented with the assistance of indigenous yeast. This is then mixed with molasses, distilled in pot stills, and aged in teak vats for six to twelve months. Generally bottled at 50 percent ABV, it is a bit harsh on its own, and as a result is most often part of a mixed drink (see page 63). Eighteenth-century Europeans incorporated arrack into punch recipes, the most popular drink of the day, almost immediately. Arracks come to life when mixed with citrus, teas, and fruit juices, amplifying the flavors of the other ingredients and bringing their best qualities to the fore (see page 148).

OTHER FRESH CANE JUICE SPIRITS

Sugarcane is a grass that takes on and expresses local terroir—aromas, flavors, and qualities of the earth, water, and flora in the vicinity where it is grown—in its distillates, like grapes do in wine. As a result, agricole rums distilled from fresh juice express more pure sugar flavors compared to those made from molasses. While traditionally consumed neat, agricole rums shine in cocktails that emphasize floral, vegetal, and savory notes or subdued tropical fruit flavors (see pages 40 and 76). They also work well in tandem with earthy, pot still rums (see page 101).

A precursor to modern Spanish-style rums, **aguardiente** is a rustic distillate made from a combination of fresh and lightly fermented cane juice. It predates industrialization of sugar cultivation in the Spanish colonies and traditionally was consumed mostly by locals. Often infused with anise to soften it (see page 60), this spirit can be a bit hot and fiery on its own. Recently, artisanal expressions that exhibit vegetal, earthy notes—the hallmark of fresh cane juice rums—have become more widely available to add their intriguing depth to more cocktails (see page 90).

Cachaça, the national spirit of Brazil, is distinguished from other fresh cane juice spirits by the use of pot still methods and a wide range of woods used in the aging process, making it especially expressive. While commercial examples are the best known, traditional cachaças still come from small village stills. Like agricole rums, they can range from floral and vegetal to funky, adding brightness as well as dry notes to a cocktail (see page 110). They pair exceptionally well with other funk-driven rums (see page 85) and add a botanical dimension to cocktails (see page 131).

Little known outside of Haiti until recently, and distilled in hundreds of small, private stills from the fresh-pressed juice of uncultivated sugarcane, **clairin** can exhibit a wide range of aromas and flavors, from soft and floral through grassy and vegetal to earthy and gravelly (see page 22).

ABV

"Alcohol by volume," or ABV, describes the alcoholic content of a beverage on a scale of 1 to 100. In the United States, most spirits are bottled at 40 percent ABV, with liqueurs in the 15 to 30 percent range, wine at 9 to 17 percent ABV, and beers typically 4.5 to 11 percent ABV, while artisanal and traditionally produced spirits can reach from 50 to 57 percent ABV. Out of the still, most spirits fall within a range of 63 to 78 percent ABV and are then diluted down to potable strength with water. This reduces the concentration of esters and congeners—vital aroma and flavor compounds—and the spirit's intensity as well as its potency.

Indispensable for more than flaming garnishes (see page 182), **overproof rums** contain more esters and congeners than other styles and correspondingly a more potent flavor. A 151-proof rum has about a 75 percent ABV, much higher than most. These rums not only help maintain a desired overall strength in a multi-ingredient cocktail, their intense flavors add depth (see page 33).

AGING

Aging allows blends to mature and develop nuance, which highlights aspects of the production and style. Wooden barrels naturally impart flavors and even some color during the aging process; repurposed barrels will also retain qualities from the spirits they previously aged. Even rums held in stainless steel tanks can benefit from the Caribbean's naturally hot and humid climate, which can accelerate the aging process and enable a relatively young spirit to achieve mature character sooner. Generally, an **unaged spirit** will reflect more of the terroir and character of the source of its distillate (see page 67).

Despite their appearance, **aged white rums** have generally spent no more than three years in a barrel, just long enough to mellow the spirit without taking on the flavor from the wood. Any color is filtered out before bottling. As a result, they retain fresher, grassier notes and are suitable for light, crisp, Latin-style cocktails (see pages 12 and 142).

Aged rums spend more time in a barrel, on average, where the brighter fruit aromas from the younger component balance out darker, earthier tones in the older. Given their range of flavors and textures, these medium-bodied rums are a great backbone upon which to build a range of cocktails, imparting notes of vanilla, burnt caramel, and toffee as well as leather, earth, and even tobacco, and they mix well with both high-ester and fresh cane juice rums (see pages 25 and 95).

Produced with the same material, fermentation, distillation, and blending techniques as the styles previously described, **extra-aged rums** spend more time in a barrel, on average seven to eight years, to emerge rounder, smoother, and more suitable for sipping neat (see page 9). Past this point, aromas and flavors from the wood dominate those of the spirit, and the product is more a reflection of the blender's style than the sugarcane. As such, these rums are best used in tandem with younger spirits in cocktails calling for a range of flavors and textures (see page 50).

Blackstrap rum, despite its dark color and extra-funky flavor (see page 157), can be aged as little as two years. Its inky coloring comes from the late-grade molasses—byproduct of cane juice boiled multiple times, to the point where it is no longer possible to extract sugar—that makes its base, sometimes helped along by a coloring agent added prior to bottling.

BLENDS, INFUSIONS, AND WASHES

Customizing spirits, whether by blending, infusing with flavors, or fat-washing, to create one's own arsenal of secret ingredients is another hallmark of Tiki. Taste and experiment to find your perfect house blend.

Navy Rum Blend: Inspired by merchant-bottler rums, this funky blend features pungent, ripe-fruit aromas and full-bodied flavors, especially useful for punches (see page 145) and smooth mixed drinks (see page 85). Combine 5 parts Demerara rum, 1 part rhum agricole ambre, and 1 part overproof Jamaican rum.

Punch Blend: This robust blend works for any old-fashioned rum punch. Combine 5 parts Barbados rum, 1 part Batavia arrack, and 1 part overproof Guyana rum.

Zombie Blend: This blend of four rums is strong enough to wake the dead (see page 25), balancing bold high-ester rum styles with earthy agricole. Combine 3 parts aged Demerara rum, 2 parts heavy pot still Jamaican rum, 1 part rhum agricole blanc, and 1½ parts 151-proof rum.

St. Lucia-Style Spiced Rum Blend: St. Lucia families are rightly proud of their spiced rum recipes—passed down over generations—used to add a spicy, high-proof spin to fruit-forward cocktails (see page 39). Combine 500 milliliters (17 ounces) Demerara rum, 200 milliliters (6¾ ounces) unaged overproof rum, 2 to 3 cinnamon sticks, ½ teaspoon whole cloves, and 2 whole star anise in a glass or nonporous, nonreactive container. Let steep at room temperature for 12 hours. Strain and decant into a clean bottle, discarding solids. Once infused, the rum will keep at room temperature in an airtight container indefinitely.

Rums have a long history of being amended by fruits and spices in order to make them more palatable, to impart a signature flavor profile or even to imbue them with medicinal properties. Recipes for infusions can be found with relevant cocktail recipes, but by all means, seize the Tiki spirit and experiment with different combinations and applications for your infused spirits. Most infusions involve simply letting the spirits steep on the aromatic ingredient, then straining; for more involved recipes, a sous vide wand (see page 112) can greatly reduce the infusion time down to a few hours—the traditional process of rhum arrangé épices could take up to eight to twelve months.

Fat-washing, a technique for infusing spirits with fat to impart a smooth, rich, and silken texture, was first utilized in the clarified milk punches popular in the late nineteenth century. While the drink has enjoyed a resurgence of popularity of late (see page 154), the labor- and material-intensive process is prohibitive, and mastering the technique can be a lengthy, frustrating, and, to the chagrin of many (myself included), expensive process. Enter Don Lee, former bartender at PDT, and his Benton's Old Fashioned, which established a simplified template for fat-washing that I still follow. Where before it was a little rough or even harsh, one sip of a fat-washed spirit will reveal its transformation into a pleasantly smooth, satiny elixir. Flavors previously undetectable are gently pushed to the fore. The experience overall is that of harmonious balance, the moment that we experience every now and again that I like to call heaven in a glass.

OTHER SPIRITS

Many spirits and spirit categories beyond molasses and cane-based rums, agricole rums, and cachaças can be employed in captivating Tiki cocktails. The tropical fruit juices, bold syrups, and bright liqueurs that characterize the genre respond to and amplify different, even unexpected qualities in agave-based spirits such as tequila and mezcal, grain spirits including whiskey and bourbon, neutral spirits such as vodka and gin, and even sake. Rich sipping brandies, including **Calvados** (see page 83), **Cognac** (see page 144), and **pisco** (see page 127), an elegantly floral Chilean brandy, also feature in a number of recipes. **Absinthe** and **pastis**, favorite tipples of nineteenth-century artists, add refreshing anise-based herbal notes as an ingredient (see page 113), swirled in the glass as a rinse (see page 64), or spritzed over drinks before serving (see page 87).

TEQUILA AND MEZCAL

Agave is one of my favorite bases for recipes in which abundant tropical fruit juices or liqueurs benefit from robust flavors for a full-bodied, intense cocktail. Where sugarcane is a grass that grows in rich, tropical soil, agave is a succulent and enjoys more desert-like conditions; however, both are terroir-expressive plants. Agave-based spirits display qualities derived from their environment, whether grassy, green vegetal notes that play like an agricole rum's, or smoky, gravelly pumice and dark, spicy earth flavors, whereas heavier-style rums are smooth and sweet.

Tequila, made exclusively from the blue agave plant in the state of Jalisco, is the more widely known. Silver tequila is unaged, retaining brighter, stronger agave flavors; reposado ("rested") has had some time to mellow (see page 88); while añejo ("aged") has spent longer in barrels, taking on some of the character of the wood itself and a generally subtler and more complex flavor. Tequila also takes well to infusions and fat-washes (see pages 118 and 135).

Tequila's cooler sister (who smokes), **mezcal** is distilled from the juice of an agave heart that has been roasted in an earthen pit, which gives the spirit its telltale smoky, earthy character. Of several varieties, espadín is especially suited to cocktailing with rums (see page 86).

WHISK(E)Y AND BOURBON

Sweet and earthy grain-based brown liquors, whiskey and bourbon both behave in a similar fashion to rum in Tiki cocktails. Whereas other **whiskeys** can be made from many different grains, most often barley, rye, corn, wheat, or a blend of these and others, by United States law, for a spirit to be called **bourbon**, its mash (the mixture of grains from which it is distilled) must be at least 51 percent corn, with the remainder most often being malted barley and rye or wheat. Other rules include using new charred wooden barrels for aging each batch—which are then often sold and used to age other spirits, including rum and tequila, which gain color, flavor, and complexity from the wood (see page 56).

Bourbon and whiskey also take well to infusions and fat-washing to add richness and mouthfeel, and to round out the spice (see page 64). In a Tiki setting, bourbon stands in for or alongside bold, full-bodied English-style rums (see page 117), contributing alcohol, body, spice, and texture. Smoky-smooth **Scotch whisky** (see page 92) is distilled mostly from malted barley; dry and peppery **rye whiskey** (see page 141), like bourbon and corn, must be made from at least 51 percent rye.

VODKA AND GIN

Vodka's characteristic crispness enables it to amplify the qualities of what you do to it or put with it. Whether mixing it with juices and liqueurs or infusing it with flavor and texture (see pages 44 and 114), vodka shines as a cold, boozy sipper.

The fiercely botanical, herbal character of **gin** makes it perhaps less of an outlier in Tiki: Juniper is actually quite close to allspice, a prominent Caribbean spice and the basis for allspice dram. **Barrel-aged gin**, popular until the mid-nineteenth century, is experiencing a resurgence today, and brings an additional element of aromatic spice as well as soft vanilla from the wood (see page 83). **Navy-strength gin** is a precursor to the later London Dry style, bottled at a higher proof and steeped with spicier botanicals that shine in multi-ingredient punches and cocktails featuring tea or fragrant citrus, such as grapefruit, lemongrass, and yuzu (see page 42)

SAKE AND SHOCHU

Distilled from rice and barley, respectively, **sake** and **shochu** can run the gamut from floral and fruity to rich, dry, and malty. While seldom mixed into cocktails in Japan, both have won a following among American and European bartenders seeking lower-ABV, softer, and subtler cocktailing spirits. Both are great options for those who enjoy sherry cocktails, infuse successfully, and can serve as an intriguing alternative to fresh cane juice spirits (see pages 54 and 132).

LIQUEURS, AMARI, AND BITTERS

As in any cocktail genre, lower-ABV liqueurs, amari, and bitters help bridge the gap between nonalcoholic juices and sweet syrups and the intense, high-ABV base spirits. Fruit-based, herbal, spiced, and even savory liqueurs add essential balance and flavor.

A Barbados rum-based infusion flavored with fragrant lime peel, ginger, cinnamon, cloves, and almonds, **falernum** is a classic Tiki ingredient that adds spice and acidity (see page 27). It's possible but rather labor-intensive to make at home, so I trust John D. Taylor's Velvet Falernum for its consistency and style. As a liqueur, falernum can be infused with botanicals, herbs, and spices (see page 68).

Named for the island, both **orange** and **blue Curaçao** contribute bitter-orange flavor, dryness, and brilliant colors to many tropical cocktails (see pages 28 and 44). Citrus pairs especially well with rum, so both spicy **Campari** (see page 36) and tart **yuzu liqueur** (see page 74) work in Tiki. **Banana liqueur** is a born companion to rum, adding dusky fruit flavors and roundness (see pages 70 and 151). A natural addition to any Tiki bar is a quality **pineapple liqueur**, the best of which adds aromatic elements but little sweetness (see page 49).

Liqueurs can also add or enhance herbal, aromatic, and spicy flavors. One of the most classic is **allspice dram**. Allspice is the dried berry of the Caribbean pimento tree, with cinnamon, clove, and nutmeg notes, and its floral, spicy qualities add depth to many cocktails (see pages 26 and 153). Like falernum and orgeat, it's possible to make at home, but I choose St. Elizabeth Allspice Dram, an Austrian import nearly as rich and tannic as bitters, or Hamilton Pimento Dram Liqueur, based on Jamaican rum, for honeyed funk.

Fragrant cinnamon, ginger, and honeyed menthol characterize bitter **Becherovka**, a Czech herbal liqueur not unlike a grown-up Jägermeister (see page 58). Both **yellow** and **green Chartreuse** bring sweet and spicy herbal flavors and their respective characteristic hues (see pages 47 and 60). A quality **ginger liqueur** harnesses the root's warm and spicy character (see page 55), which works with everything. **Suze**, a French aperitif flavored with gentian root (one of the main ingredients in bitters), tastes tart, fragrant, and vegetal-green at the same time (see page 78).

Savory flavors contribute welcome balance to rich spirits and sugary syrups. **Crème de cacao** complements dark, rum-based drinks, adding a refreshingly dry element and depth of flavor (see page 92). Spice as true heat from **chile liqueur** adds excitement and brings out rum's grassy, vegetal character (see pages 46 and 142). Earthy **coffee liqueur** (see page 102) and tangy **tamarind liqueur** (see page 93) both complement the naturally round, sweet flavors in heavier-bodied Tiki spirits.

Amari are bitter, herbal liqueurs from the Italian beverage culture—essentially bitters in long form and developed as digestifs to enjoy at the conclusion of a meal. Neutral spirits steeped in botanicals and herbs, amari range from floral and nutty to earthy and tannic, making them a welcome addition to multi-ingredient cocktails, where they can play a significant role in grounding and unifying the elements of a drink.

Dark, bracing, and bitter, with faint licorice and menthol notes, **fernet** has become a bartender favorite for its intensity, which when incorporated thoughtfully into a cocktail opens up to reveal cocoa, hazelnut, and dark earth (see page 60). Herbaceous and woody, **Fernet Vallet** is made from a maceration of aromatic plants, roots, and spices, including cinnamon, clove, gentian root, and cardamom (see page 95). The heavy emphasis on spices makes it an accessible and versatile Tiki ingredient, as does the menthol character of **Fernet Menta** (see page 56). The elegant, herbal, and artichoke-reliant **Cynar** has a bracing vegetal character, but doesn't actually taste like artichokes (see page 90). Technically, it's a spicy schnapps, but guilty pleasure **Jägermeister** functions like an amaro in Tiki cocktails (see page 109), adding high-proof bitter herbal notes and body, so if there's a bottle buried in the freezer since your last college party, here's its chance.

An indispensible bar tool since its release in 1824, **Angostura bitters** are an alcoholic infusion of barks and herbs, often featuring gentian root, and considered the ultimate flavor enhancer for cocktails (think salt and pepper for the bar). Their intensity

makes them especially useful for balancing sweet and complex Tiki cocktails. **Peychaud's Bitters**, created in 1830s New Orleans, use anise as the defining flavor over gentian, with softer baking-spice notes that pair beautifully with pineapple and other tropical flavors. Two **Tiki bitters**, both featuring cinnamon, allspice, and other Caribbean spices warrant inclusion: floral **El Guapo Bitters Polynesian Kiss** incorporate passion fruit, guava, and coconut, while **Bittermens 'Elemakule Tiki Bitters** were inspired by falernum, with bright spice without the intensity of gentian root (see page 22). The bright citrus aromas and leathery notes in **cardamom bitters** add depth to spirit-forward cocktails (see page 44) while lengthening the finish. A marriage of savory chocolate and spices, **mole bitters** make a natural companion for mezcal or Demerara rums—try the Bitter End Mexican Mole Bitters or Bittermens Xocolatl Mole Bitters to add acidity and depth to cocktails based on earthier spirits or bitter liqueurs (see page 93).

INGREDIENTS

ICE

While it may not seem like the most vital ingredient in a successful cocktail, this oft-overlooked element serves two distinct and indispensable functions—to chill down the cocktail before drinking and to dilute the cocktail even a tiny amount through the introduction of water while mixing. Different styles of ice are best depending on the method used to prepare, serve, and garnish the drink. Size matters: Generally, finer ice will dilute the drink faster, and is best suited for more spirit-forward recipes, in order to facilitate mellowing the drink at a steady, gentle pace.

Cubes are best when shaking a Daiquiri-style drink for efficient dilution, or to serve a drink over, when slower dilution is required. For lower-ABV cocktails or those with delicate and nuanced flavors, it is important to avoid over-dilution. In cases like these, light ice, only three to four cubes depending on their size, or roughly half the amount of ice that you would ordinarily use is the best way to go.

Pebbled ice, or crushed, nugget, or pellet ice, is essential to Cobbler and julep-style drinks that are high in alcohol content or are prepared by swizzling. Reasonably priced countertop ice makers are worth considering if you make a lot of cocktails with a flash blender. Crushing ice by hand with a canvas Lewis bag and wooden mallet works just as well in a glamorous, old-school way (for classic martinis, too), provided you're happy to employ a little more elbow grease.

Shaved ice is produced by running cubed ice through an ice chipper—which is fun if also a tad noisy. A countertop ice chipper is another worthwhile investment if you enjoy more elaborate ice garnishes, such as an ice cone (see page 32). As the name suggests, an ice cone involves molding shaved ice into a conical shape with a hole through the center for a straw. Beachbum Berry makes a straightforward mold.

Ice can take on an even bigger role in large-format communal drinks (see page 140). Given that a punch might be set out for the duration of your party, some savvy hosts employ a single, large block of ice, rather than many small ice cubes, to keep it as cold as possible without losing too much flavor to unwanted dilution and to add another striking visual element to the punch. Two common examples are a block or ring: Freeze water in a silicone mold, food-storage container, mixing bowl, or baking dish. To avoid having to chunk up a brand-new block, choose a mold that will not take up more than one-third of your vessel. If you prefer the look of a ring, freeze water in a Bundt or ring pan—if it has a pattern stamped into it, even better. Silicone molds for spheres or blocky cubes can be good for vessels too narrow or shallow for a single block or ring. Freeze flavorful garnishes like citrus wheels, edible flowers, and cherries or pineapple chunks inside ice for added flourish.

Finally, keep in mind that ice absorbs the aromas and flavors of its environment, so make certain that you regularly clean and deodorize your trays with a solution of water and baking soda or a rinse of vinegar. If possible, dedicate a section of your freezer for cocktail ice only, not to be shared with leftovers or food storage. I use a sealable box for my ice and keep baking soda in my freezer as an added precaution.

FRUIT JUICES AND PUREES

By all means, those lucky enough to live anywhere blessed with available local, ripe tropical fruit can make fresh juices and fruit purees whenever possible, but that's not many of us. Commercial lemon and lime juices and most orange juices should be avoided entirely—here, fresh truly is the only acceptable option for delicious cocktails. While fresh pineapple isn't difficult to juice, it is laborious, and even the finickiest bartender I know will swear by Dole's reliable brightness of flavor. The Perfect Puree of Napa Valley is my go-to source for tropical or specialty frozen fruit purees. Many can be found online or at specialty stores; check in Asian, Caribbean, or Latin markets.

SUGAR AND SYRUPS

There are a number of ways to sweeten a cocktail, and different sugars will impart a different mouthfeel in addition to different flavors. Most bars rely on simple syrup for speed and consistency, even in their Daiquiris; however, the traditional preparation, and my recipe (see page 16), calls for granulated sugar. In a shaken drink, sugar won't totally dissolve, existing instead as tiny particles held in suspension, giving the drink a subtle but distinct effervescent quality. Syrups do dissolve, lending a smoother, if heavier, texture and pleasing body to the finished cocktail.

Syrups may be a cocktail maker's best secret weapon because they can be kept readily at hand, mix quickly and evenly into cocktails, and enable easy experimentation to create new and customized cocktails. Recipes for specialty syrups abound (and follow, below); however, there are widely available brands that professionals and Tiki experts alike trust for their quality and consistency. Reàl Cocktail Ingredients and Small Hand Foods both make a range of tropical fruit–infused syrups, including banana, mango, and passion fruit. Exotic fruit and nut flavors, like papaya, pistachio, and macadamia nut, can be found from Amoretti, Hella Cocktail Co., Monin, or Torani.

Simple syrup is a classic 1:1 combination of sugar and water that scales up easily to any volume needed. Heat 1 cup water in a small saucepan over medium-high heat. Once it comes to a boil, add the sugar and stir briskly to dissolve completely. The syrup is done when the liquid is clear, about 5 minutes. Brush the inside of the saucepan with a wet pastry brush as needed to remove sugar crystals as they form. Remove from heat and let cool to room temperature. Keep in the refrigerator for 3 to 4 weeks.

Rich syrup is a favorite of many bartenders since it adds more sweetness by volume and gives the drink an even fuller body. Double the amount of sugar in the simple syrup recipe, keeping a close eye on crystallization while simmering. Keep in the refrigerator for up to 2 weeks.

Demerara syrup has an earthy flavor and more vibrant body, making it ideal for drinks with a dark spirit base. Since the golden brown grains of Demerara sugar are larger than granulated sugar crystals, the syrup, while flavorful, is actually less sweet than simple syrup. Keep in the refrigerator for 3 to 4 weeks.

Cane syrup, also known as *sirop de canne*, is essential for a proper Ti' Punch (see page 14) and has a fresh, raw quality. Made from fresh-pressed cane juice, cane sugar retains some of the vegetal terroir from the sugarcane. Variations add orange zest, cinnamon sticks, vanilla beans, whole cloves, or allspice berries, and even bay leaves. Keep in the refrigerator for 3 to 4 weeks.

Vanilla syrup adds smooth, creamy sweetness to drinks with any dark or spiced base in one of two ways: Add up to 1 tablespoon vanilla extract to water in Demerara syrup recipe. For a more authentic style found in classic Tiki bars, pour hot simple syrup over 1 whole vanilla bean, split lengthwise, in a glass jar or bottle and let cool. Keep syrup made with extract in the refrigerator for up to 2 weeks; syrup made with a whole vanilla bean will keep in the refrigerator for 1 week.

Honey syrup also lends a creamy mouthfeel, with honey's added floral and herbal notes. Use the same 1:1 ratio for simple syrup with any variety of honey—I like clover or buckwheat, but try your local favorite. Add a generous pinch of sea salt to the water for **salted honey syrup**; the spices from spiced syrup (see page 176) for a **spiced honey syrup** variation; or an equal volume of thawed passion fruit puree for **passion fruit–honey syrup**. Keep in the refrigerator for up to 2 weeks.

Toasted coconut syrup adds elegant, exotic flavor and is what I'll often reach for first when a recipe calls for coconut cream. Toast ½ cup unsweetened coconut in a dry skillet over medium-low heat until fragrant and light golden brown. Combine toasted coconut with 1 cup coconut water and 1 cup honey and follow the simple syrup recipe, simmering the mixture for about 30 minutes. Let cool, then strain and discard solids. Use granulated sugar in place of honey for a brighter, sweeter version. Keep in the refrigerator for up to 2 weeks.

Don's Mix is a beloved Tiki ingredient invented by the master at balancing sweet and sour, Don the Beachcomber himself, for adding mellow sweetness and acidity to complex cocktails. Combine 1 part cinnamon-honey syrup (omit cloves from spiced honey syrup, see page 176 and below) with 1 part fresh grapefruit juice. Keep in the refrigerator for up to 2 weeks.

Spiced syrup includes warm, aromatic flavors that pair beautifully with funky rums and rhum agricoles. Heat 3 to 4 cinnamon sticks in a dry skillet over medium-low heat until toasted and fragrant (they may give off a little smoke). Add cinnamon and ½ teaspoon whole cloves to simple syrup recipe once it comes to a simmer. Strain and discard the spices from cooled syrup. Omit cloves for a pure **cinnamon syrup** variation. Keep in the refrigerator for up to 2 weeks.

Ginger syrup brings exotic warmth that works well with any spirit and most fruit juices. Follow the simple syrup recipe, adding up to 4 ounces fresh ginger, peeled and sliced into thin coins, once it comes to a simmer. Let steep for 45 minutes before straining and discarding solids. Ginger's wild cousins, aromatic galangal and earthy turmeric, also make delicious syrups. Keep in the refrigerator for up to 2 weeks.

Tea syrup combines rich mouthfeel with the sharp flavors of black or green teas, or herbal tisanes. Brew according to your favorite method—it should be strong but not tannic or bitter. Follow the simple syrup recipe, using freshly brewed tea or tisane in place of water. Bold black teas like Earl Grey; grassy green tea; fragrant herbal blends like hibiscus and rooibos; and aromatic herbs such as lemongrass and peppermint all make delicious and versatile syrups. Keep in the refrigerator for up to 2 weeks.

Coffee syrup is excellent in any cocktail calling for cacao notes, adding sweetness along with rich, round flavors, as well as acidity and tannin. Follow the simple syrup recipe, using brewed coffee in place of water. Coffee lovers can double-brew their coffee (use half the usual amount of water) for an even stronger, more potent flavor. I suggest darker single-origin beans from Mexico, Guatemala, or Sumatra, or a blend incorporating one or more of these for consistency and flavor. Keep in the refrigerator for up to 2 weeks.

Pineapple syrup is one of my personal favorites, which I frequently use in place of simple syrup to give any cocktail an extra tropical gloss. Because of the volume of the fruit, I usually start with a double batch of simple syrup—2 cups each of sugar and water. Cut a ripe pineapple in half and half again lengthwise; then peel, core, and cube one quarter. You should have about 2 cups chopped pineapple. In an airtight glass or nonporous, nonreactive container, combine simple syrup and pineapple, cover, and let steep in the refrigerator for 48 hours, then strain and discard solids. Keep in the refrigerator for up to 2 weeks.

Orgeat is an almond-based syrup and a truly classical Tiki ingredient, pivotal to a true Mai Tai (see page 28). Essentially a concentrated form of horchata, its floral aromas and subtle, lightly caramelized sugars make orgeat popular in confectionary and baking as well as a great natural bedfellow for the earthy, funky flavors in Caribbean rum. While one can make one's own orgeat at home (see page 102 for Nathan Hazard's macadamia nut variation), it's an ingredient I am happy to purchase. L'Orgeat, Small Hand Foods, and Beachbum Berry all make excellent and widely available versions.

TOOLS AND EQUIPMENT

BARWARE

Proper tools play a hugely important role in mixing drinks effectively and getting the desired result. Tiki and tropical drinks come in a number of formats, and while most employ traditional cocktail equipment, some are most successful when made with specific tools. In addition to being the means to make fantastic drinks, barware also provides an opportunity to add personality to your cocktailing: Consider colored finishes, unconventional materials and embellishments, and interpreting Tiki's natural retro-tropical character through your own style. Have fun curating your collection and discovering inspiration in the details.

Jiggers and **measures** are indispensable to get the best results. There are a number of styles from which to choose, though American and Japanese are the easiest to find. The former is a bit bulkier; the latter, slimmer and easier to handle, though less tolerant of errors in measuring as they are designed for professionals who have honed their skills and precision through practice. Look for a graduated or stepped design that goes down to ⅛ ounce—if clear, all the better. For added precision, consider adding a set of measuring spoons to your cocktail kit. Look for standard and metric measures.

Muddlers break up fruit and plant matter for improved integration while shaking. Most muddlers are made from maple or walnut wood, but if you make large batches of cocktails, consider one in kitchen-grade plastic. The larger surface area will help you get your work done faster, plus it is easier to clean and virtually indestructible. Mint should be muddled lightly to prevent releasing bitter compounds. Similar care should be taken when muddling citrus to focus on the flesh as opposed to the peel—a notable exception being the adorable kumquat, as its deliciously aromatic skin adds great flavor when muddled. Other fruit and vegetables require less gentleness.

Swizzle sticks were not shaped by human hands; the perfectly splay-end stirrers are cut from *Quararibea turbinata*, also known as the swizzle stick tree, an aromatic evergreen from the Caribbean whose branches naturally grow in radial spokes. The stick can be used to mix, gently muddle citrus and plant matter, and to churn pebbled ice to chill down a drink. In the French Antilles, it is known as a *baton-lele* and is the traditional tool used in the preparation of Ti' Punch (see page 14).

Bar spoons stir mixtures that do not contain citrus or require shaking to swizzle (or agitate)—a Mojito, Cobbler, or Swizzle-style drink. There are a number of lengths and sizes to consider, as well as styles that have picks or muddlers on the blunt end for additional functionality. A bar spoon traditionally holds 1 teaspoon (about 5 milliliters of liquid) and can also be used as a handy measure.

Mixing glasses can be found in any number of sizes and styles—thin-walled and utilitarian, embossed with bold patterns, or etched with elegant designs. As a beautiful visual element for your bar, these are a great place to splurge. Stainless steel mixing tins, a modern take on the stainless steel-and-glass Boston shaker, emphasize function over fashion and are more effective in chilling cocktails efficiently.

Shakers come into play when vigorous agitation is required to combine citrus, sugar, and other ingredients with spirits and ice to chill and aerate. Cobblers, sometimes called Japanese shakers, are smaller and will chill a drink faster, making them excellent for single-serve pours. A Boston shaker consists of two tins, ideally of heavier gauge metal—those made of thinner metals are prone to fusing, becoming VERY difficult to separate—one small enough to fit snugly into the larger to form a sealed chamber. The larger cup can be used with wand-style flash blenders. A pint glass can stand in for the smaller cup, but will chill the drink less effectively.

Strainers, likewise, come in a number of styles. I prefer the Koriko Hawthorne Strainer from Cocktail Kingdom or OXO's stainless steel model—both are as attractive and stylish as they are durable. **Hawthorne strainers** fit snugly into the top of a mixing tin, with holes around the perimeter that allows liquid to flow from the shaker. This style uses a spring coil that responds to your grip to slow or speed the rate of flow from the shaker and keeps ice, fruit pieces, or herbs out of drinks served up or over ice. **Fine-mesh strainers,** as the name suggests, catch smaller particles and are essential for serving clean, crisp sours.

Countertop blenders offer power, speed, versatility of application, and durability. Vitamix is generally acknowledged for making the best model in this category, and for fans of frozen drinks (and juices, smoothies, and pureed sauces or soups) it's a worthwhile investment for a serious piece of equipment.

Wand-style **stand mixers** or **flash blenders** come in a range of sizes and styles from commercial-grade with multiple wands to smaller models for home use. Prominent in both classic and contemporary Tiki bars, flash blenders are prized for their speed, efficiency, and consistency. Unlike a pitcher-style blender, it doesn't puree; the wand agitates and aerates drinks at high speeds (you'll never have a better milkshake). Hamilton Beach makes a couple of reliable models that are more portable and less expensive than a KitchenAid stand mixer or Vitamix.

Though it may seem like a luxury, when space or time is a consideration, a **sous vide wand** or machine can save both. Many professionals employ these to infuse spirits with rich, potent flavors quickly and evenly, and the same can apply at home. The simplest consist of little more than a programmable, waterproof heating element that clips to the side of a deep pot, but more advanced models are widely available. A vacuum sealer and bags make for no-fear infusions, securely enclosing your spirits, syrups, and spices.

GLASSWARE AND VESSELS

Even more than barware, here is where Tiki truly shines as a way to express one's personality. Tiki arguably has a well-established aesthetic, combining kitsch, Polynesian fantasy, and nostalgia—most cocktails can be built and served in the same shapes as neat pours, mixed drinks, and martinis, with a few specific themed vessels for fun. Current tropical trends make this a great time to stock and style a Tiki bar, whether your style leans more toward vintage surf shack, Caribbean colonial, or chic midcentury modern.

The most glamorous way to serve up classic Daiquiris and Tiki drinks is in a **coupe,** wide-mouthed stemmed glasses with generous curves where martini glasses have straight lines and sharp angles. Combining retro elegance with practicality, the **Nick and Nora** glass is a sleek and nearly slosh-proof sipper halfway between a coupe and martini glass (see page 45).

Rocks glasses hold neat pours and short drinks over ice. Heavy-bottomed and satisfying to hold, these can be straight-sided, tapered, or round, very clean or ornate with cut glass or metal details. Singles, for sipping, and doubles, which can hold large ice cubes, cones, or spheres, are both useful in a well-stocked Tiki bar.

Put a tapered rocks glass on a short foot and behold the voluptuous **snifter**. The unique shape's narrow mouth focuses the vapors coming off the spirit, making small snifters ideal for savoring quality rums and agricoles. Larger ones are great options for mixed and frozen drinks or even as a small bowl for two.

A **Collins glass**, also called a highball, or cooler, is the classic choice for long drinks. Its tall shape holds plenty of ice, but the narrow mouth keeps evaporation to a minimum, and it's easy to hold. They come with decorative glazing, colorful designs, and fun etching or as minimalist columns to suit your style. The sleek curves of a stainless steel **swizzle cup** come straight out of a sixties space-age fantasy and are ideal for leisurely sipping higher-proof cocktails (see page 84)

The curiously shaped **Pearl Diver** was a stylish mainstay in midcentury Tiki bars now roaring back into vogue and wide availability, after decades of near obscurity. Named after the classic Tiki cocktail, the eye-catching and instantly Instagrammable glass serves any tall drink (see page 139).

The **hurricane** holds larger-volume drinks and those calling for a dramatic presentation. They're voluminous enough to hold large or frozen cocktails and gracefully balance their height with a rounded mouth and a heavy foot, sometimes on a short stem. A generous wine glass, beer glass, or large water goblet could stand in.

When it comes to communicating an aesthetic, it's hard to beat a **Tiki mug**, the now-iconic kitschy ceramic collectibles sold to tourists the world over. Whether you enjoy the tropical fantasy or consider it tacky at best and cultural appropriation at worst, there's probably a Tiki mug out there to suit your style. By now, pop culture has firmly embraced Tiki, filling the market with superheroes, classic movie monsters, and figures from literature and politics besides the standard oceanic, skull-shaped, and island-idol mugs. In truth, any food-safe, watertight vessel counts as a Tiki mug if holding a Tiki drink.

Refreshingly, **Tiki bowls** are exactly what they sound like, vessels for more than one person actually to drink from, but not full-sized punch bowls from which to portion out servings. The classic volcano design (see page 146) features a wide round bowl

on a foot with a central pillar; atop that pillar is a shallow bowl ideal for a flaming garnish. As with Tiki mugs, any food-safe, watertight vessel from which four to six people can comfortably drink (long straws help) can function as a creative and stylish Tiki bowl.

Whether minimalist, pedestal-style, or shaped, made of cut glass, hammered metal, or plastic, a successful punch bowl combines beauty, drama, and convenience to create a striking visual statement while serving a group easily. Whether for special occasions or weekly parties, a **punch bowl** means a celebration, so this is the place to go all out and have fun. Most styles come with matching cups, but any small tumbler or handled cup will do. When entertaining outdoors, consider a cistern dispenser on a stand (see page 159).

Pitchers will serve groups with more portability than a punch bowl (see page 161). Use any punch or double any bowl recipe and pour over citrus wheels or muddled fruit and herbs. Top with large ice cubes and stir to mix with a swizzle stick.

Sometimes only the real thing will do. **Young coconuts** make a fresh vessel (see page 116) for tropical drinks. Bore holes through the top with an ice pick or sharp knife to drain the coconut water. Refill the shell with a funnel and serve with a straw. Keep chilled and covered or mist periodically to avoid drying out.

GARNISHES AND FINISHING TOUCHES

Tiki is genuinely one of the most culinary of cocktail genres, balancing strong flavors and textures, and as such it prioritizes its garnishes. The fruit, floral, herbal, or spice element (or some combination thereof) that finishes a Tiki cocktail is never an afterthought or arbitrary decoration. Garnishes fulfill an essential function, engaging all five senses to complete the drink.

While many brilliant and creative modern mixologists devise elaborate edible garnishes that border on hors d'oeuvres in your drink, I am unapologetically classical in my tastes (at least for garnishes), loyal in most cases to the adage, "What grows together, goes together."

Fruit, especially citrus, adds flavor, fragrance, and acidity at once. Fresh lime, lemon, or orange **zest** can be grated with a rasp, scored in thin ribbons by a zester, or cut in wide strips by a vegetable peeler, contributing aroma and flavor without adding liquid. For **twists** or pieces of peel thick enough to cut into shapes or thread onto a skewer, cut the whole fruit into wheels or sections, then remove the flesh from the inside, leaving the pith and peel intact, and slice.

A citrus **disc** is one of the earliest cocktail garnishes, basically a slice of peel carrying oils from the zest without juice from the flesh. To cut, use a sharp paring knife to slice a silver dollar-sized circle of peel and pith from the outside edge of the lime or other citrus fruit, taking as little of the flesh as possible. A **citrus wheel**, by contrast, is a complete cross-section of the fruit, which does include the flesh and its juice. **Scoring** citrus wedges, wheels, halves, or shells with a channel knife cuts long, shallow ruts through the peel into the pith, activating and releasing aromatic compounds—try this before muddling. Keep in mind you can score or zest fruit before juicing, but not after.

After juicing a halved lime, you're left with the **shell**, which can still contribute oils and fragrance. A **flaming lime shell** is Tiki at its most theatrical—a sure sign something extraordinary is heading your way. While any drink can, in theory, be adorned with a flaming garnish, they work best on cocktails served on pebbled or crushed ice for stability or as a centerpiece to Tiki bowls (see page 146). With a sharp knife, remove the flesh from the interior of a halved lime, leaving the peel intact, to create a bowl or cup shape. Soak a sugar cube with 151-proof rum, add it to the empty lime shell, place the shell in the drink, and top with another splash of rum. Just before serving, carefully ignite with a chef's torch or long match (do not use a lighter). As shown on page 121, sprinkling ground cinnamon over the flame will create impressive, if brief, sparks.

Whenever working with open flame of any kind, and most especially around higher proof alcohol, always observe caution. It is for good reason that 151-proof rum is not allowed aboard aircraft: If a bottle were to light, it would explode. Always work in a well-ventilated area away from flammable materials. Avoid overly loose clothing, roll up your sleeves, and tie your hair back. Always have a working fire extinguisher close by (and know how to use it). When ready, pour the rum first, then seal and put away the bottle before introducing flame—never attempt to light the garnish at the same time.

Dehydrated citrus wheels add a striking visual element as well as a subtler, more concentrated flavor to drinks and punches, especially as the liquid starts to rehydrate the dried fruit. Preheat your oven to 200°F and slice fruit into ¼-inch-thick wheels. Arrange slices in a single layer on a wire rack set on a baking sheet and bake until dry to the touch, turning occasionally, about 2 to 3 hours for lemon, lime, or blood oranges, and up to 4½ hours for larger fruit.

Arguably, the noncitrus fruit best suited to garnish Tiki cocktails has to be pineapple. With a sharp chef's knife, slice thin slices or rounds from a ripe pineapple, leaving peel and core intact; known as a **pineapple chip**, these are usually pliable enough to fit into a round glass and will add a subtle sweetness to the cocktail. Peel and cut **wedges** from thicker slices to garnish the edge of a glass or mug. To **dehydrate pineapple**, preheat oven to 225ºF. Peel and remove eyes from 1 ripe pineapple, then thinly slice crosswise and cut into desired shape. Place fruit in a single layer on a wire rack set in a baking sheet and bake, turning once, until dried to the touch and lightly golden brown, about 1 hour.

With their striking shape and bright green hue, **pineapple spears** or **leaves** are one of the most emblematic Tiki garnishes. The sure test of a ripe pineapple is to tug on the spears at the very top of the crown: If they release easily, the fruit is ripe, and you've got a ready, elegant garnish. While the spears slide easily into any rocks or Collins glass, a miniature clothespin is a clever and practical way to clip and fan out the leaves to the side of a coupe.

Broad, glossy green, and easy to cut into shapes or tie, **banana leaves** are another popular tropical garnish; practical, too, since they can be kept frozen and thawed before use without compromising their color or texture. Their flexibility comes from moisture, so keep them wet to prevent brittleness or breakage. Source them online or at specialty Asian grocers— Thai banana leaves give off a lovely coconut-almond aroma and are easier to cut into thin ribbons to tie around your glass.

Mint is the unsung workhorse of botanical herbs. Its bright freshness is a natural match for both dark spirits and citrus—think juleps and Mojitos. There are few Tiki cocktails that a simple sprig of fresh mint won't enhance.

Tiki lovers can also look to their spice cabinets for delicious and versatile garnishes, including **nutmeg**, **cinnamon sticks**, and **star anise**. Like citrus zest,

grating fresh nutmeg releases fragrant compounds that add warm, aromatic spice notes on top of a cocktail or punch. Toasting whole spices in a dry skillet until lightly colored and fragrant is another way to engage the spices' aromatic oils before adding them to a cocktail (try charring the end of a cinnamon stick until just blackened for extra smoky flavor).

An atomizer or mister lets you **spritz** the herbal spirit over individual glasses before serving. Another martini technique often used with vermouth, a **rinse** accomplishes much the same thing: Splash a small amount of liqueur into the glass and swirl to coat, then toss. Only the tiny amount left clinging to the sides of the glass makes it into the actual drink.

Befitting Tiki's tropical origins, **edible flowers** make a gorgeous and very authentic finishing touch for many cocktails, bowls, and punches. Beautiful, fragrant, and evocative, like the best recipe ingredients, they engage all five senses as well as the imagination. Besides magenta and white orchids, options include exotic hibiscus and jasmine, peppery arugula flowers, and less tropical blossoms such as marigolds, nasturtiums, pansies, and violets that, nonetheless, look beautiful in a punch bowl. Fresh edible flowers can be sourced online and found at many farmers' markets during spring and summer.

Not all details need to serve multisensory functions— and in Tiki, more is definitely more. Seek out interesting **cocktail picks** and **stirrers**; use bendy or metal **straws** to answer a practical question, "How do I drink this?" with a fun and whimsical way to enjoy the cocktail. And never let it be said that I am too good for the immortal **paper umbrella**. No matter how modern or stylish, a not-too-serious sense of fun and playfulness is at the heart of Tiki and enlivens the whole experience.

Index

(Page references in *italics* refer to illustrations.)

Acknowledgments

There are many individuals who have played a meaningful role in assisting me to bring this book from idea to reality. Thanks to my friends and family, especially those who helped me in too many ways to count on the way to writing this book: Richard Killeaney, Christiana Caro, Rory Berthiaume, Rachel Warner, Zave Martohardjono, Dan Gotkin, and Nicole Taylor. Thank you to my friends in the industry who contributed recipes for this book: Laura Bishop, Will Elliott, Dani DeLuna, Nathan Hazard, Karen Fu, Jason Alexander, Ean Bancroft, and Karen Jarman. To my colleagues in the spirits and hospitality industries, who gave me inspiration, mentorship, and support to follow my dream of becoming a top-notch bar and spirits professional: Katrine Polari, Allison Stuart, Luke and Lurie Jackson, Michael Jacober, Gabe McMackin, Del Pedro, Brother Cleve, Dane Risch, Austin Hartman, Tom Roughton, Nicholas Pelis, and many more.

There are, of course, the countless bars and restaurants where I cut my teeth and honed my craft, including Do or Dine, The Finch, and Hart's and, most important of all, Glady's Caribbean, where I got my big break and acquired my passion for rum. To all the guests I had the pleasure to serve over the years, in Brooklyn and elsewhere, who inspired me to serve the best cocktails and give the best hospitality I could muster, and the bars who graciously lent me space to capture the images for my book—and rums to enjoy after a long day of shooting—King Tai and Super Power. Meanwhile, Colina Cuervo and Berg'n housed and fed me on the many ocassions when I needed a place to work away from home.

It bears mentioning that this book would not have been possible without Noah Fecks, whose photography is featured here and who inspired me to take a shot at writing my first book; my editor, Jono Jarrett, who helped me to bring form and shape to my ideas; Christopher Spaulding, my stylist, for his impeccable taste and wit; and Rizzoli, for publishing this book.

Finally, I owe a big thank you to my sister, Tamika Mustipher, who was there from the beginning, encouraging and celebrating my accomplishments every step of the way, while reminding me to enjoy the journey and to "look 'em in the eye and give them what they want."

Shannon Mustipher is a spirits educator, cocktail consultant, and expert on the topic of rum and cane spirits. In 2014, she became the Beverage Director of Glady's Caribbean in Brooklyn, and has poured cocktails in settings ranging from neighborhood pubs to Michelin-starred restaurants. In addition to working with a number of spirits brands across a range of categories, she is one of the founding members of Women Leading Rum, an organization dedicated to providing education and professional development for industry and trade professionals. In 2018, she launched Women Who Tiki, a tropical cocktail-centric pop up that gathers a team of women bartenders to share their talents and collaborate on creating a one-night-only experience, which has been featured at Rumba Seattle, Tiki Oasis, and New York Cocktail Expo's Rum Room.

Shannon's writing, cocktail recipes, and opinions have been featured in a number of publications, including Punch.com, GQ.com, Liquor.com, *New York* Magazine, Design Sponge, and the Huffington Post, and she has been a panelist and presenter at Bar Convent Brooklyn, NY Rum Fest, the Museum of Food and Drink, and Food Book Fair NYC.